THE REVISED ORDINANCES

OF THE

CITY OF DETROIT

FOR THE YEAR 1871,

REVISED AND PUBLISHED

BY ORDER OF THE COMMON COUNCIL.

DETROIT:
FREE PRESS BOOK AND JOB PRINTING HOUSE.
1871.

NOTE.

In accordance with the instructions of the Common Council, the City Attorney and City Clerk have prepared a revision of the Ordinances of the City of Detroit, containing all the Ordinances now in force. The last revision was made in 1863. It will be seen that there have been radical and numerous changes in our municipal laws since that date.

Detroit, February 1, 1871.

CONTENTS.

TITLE I.

CITY OFFICERS.

TITLE II.

TAXES AND ASSESSMENTS.

TITLE III.

STREETS, ALLEYS AND PUBLIC PLACES.

TITLE IV.

STREET RAILWAYS, RAILROADS, STEAMBOATS AND VESSELS.

TITLE V.

SEWERS.

TITLE VI.

MARKETS AND SALES.

TITLE VII.

THE PUBLIC HEALTH.

TITLE VIII.

THE PUBLIC PEACE.

TITLE IX.

THE RECORDER'S COURT.

TITLE X.

PREVENTION OF FIRES.

TITLE XI.

RESTRAINING ANIMALS.

TITLE XII.

HACKS, DRAYS AND PORTERS.

TITLE XIII.

PLACES OF AMUSEMENT AND RECREATION.

TITLE XIV.

LICENSES.

TITLE XV.

MISCELLANEOUS.

REVISED ORDINANCES

OF

THE CITY OF DETROIT.

TITLE I.

CITY OFFICERS.

CHAPTER 1.

OFFICIAL BONDS.

[Ordinance Approved November 15, 1869.]

SECTION 1. The official bonds of officers of the city shall be required in the following named amounts, to wit:

City Controller, in the sum of thirty thousand dollars.

City Clerk, in the sum of three thousand dollars.

City Attorney, in the sum of two thousand dollars.

City Counselor, in the sum of five thousand dollars.

City Treasurer, in the sum of two hundred thousand dollars.

City Surveyor, in the sum of five thousand dollars.

Director of the Poor, in the sum of five thousand dollars.

Receiver of Taxes, in the sum of fifty thousand dollars.

City Assessor, in the sum of twenty-five thousand dollars.

Superintendent of House of Correction, in the sum of twenty-five thousand dollars.

Clerk of the Recorder's Court, in the sum of three thousand dollars.

City Collector, in the sum of ten thousand dollars.

Inspector of Gas Meters, in the sum of two thousand dollars.

Inspectors of Firewood, in the sum of one thousand dollars.

Harbor Master, in the sum of two thousand dollars.

Clerk of the Market, in the sum of five thousand dollars.

Inspector of Chimneys, in the sum of two thousand dollars.

Weighmasters, in the sum of two thousand dollars.

Ward Collectors, in the sum of two thousand dollars, and such additional sums as shall make the entire bonds double the amount of the tax to be collected.

Clerk of the Police Court, in the sum of two thousand dollars.

City Sexton, in the sum of five thousand dollars.

Superintendent of Parks, in the sum of two thousand dollars.

Street Commissioners, in the sum of three thousand dollars.

Pound Masters, in the sum of three thousand dollars.

Constables, in the sum of two thousand dollars.

Overseers of Highways, in the sum of two thousand dollars.

Deputy Director of the Poor, in the sum of two thousand dollars.

City Physicians, in the sum of two thousand dollars.

Scavengers, in the sum of five hundred dollars.

CHAPTER 2.

ALDERMEN.

[Ordinance Approved February 14, 1870.]

SECTION 1. Each Alderman shall be paid the sum of one dollar and fifty cents per diem for each and every regular session of the Council at which he is in attendance from the opening to the close of such session, or excused from full attendance. The same shall be paid by warrant of the Controller upon the Contingent fund, upon the Clerk's certificate of the attendance of any Alderman. [*As amended by Ordinance approved October 20, 1870.*]

SEC. 2. It shall be the duty of each and every Alderman to attend each and every session of the Common Council, whether regular or special, unless prevented by absence from the city, sickness, or other good or sufficient cause.

SEC. 3. No Alderman who is present at any session of the Council, shall retire or absent himself therefrom until the Council meeting is adjourned; and every Alderman shall vote upon any question upon which a vote is taken, unless interested in said question; and no Alderman, during any session of the Council at which he is present, shall violate or disobey any rule or regulation adopted by the Council, or be guilty of any disorderly or offensive conduct, either by word or act.

SEC. 4. It shall be the duty of the Captain or Sergeant of Police, upon being directed by the Common Council, to go to any Alderman who is absent from a session of the Council, and, unless an excuse satisfactory to the Captain or Sergeant of Police is given, to arrest such Alderman and bring him before the Council, and retain him in custody until the President or Council direct his release.

SEC. 5. Any Alderman who fails to perform the duties herein provided for, or who violates any of the provisions of this Ordinance, shall be subject to a reprimand by the President, or the forfeiture of his pay for such period as the Council shall determine, or both, when so directed by a vote of a majority of the Common Council.

CHAPTER 3.

RECORDER.

[Ordinance Approved October 25, 1866.]

SECTION 1. The vacancy now existing in the office of Recorder of said City shall be filled at the annual City election, to be held on the sixth day of November, A. D. 1866, by the election of a person duly qualified to fill such vacancy, who shall hold said office of Recorder of said City for the residue of the official term. Notice of the filling of said vacancy, at said election, shall be given by the Clerk of said City, to be published in two or more daily newspapers of said City, at least four days prior to the said sixth day of November.

SEC. 2. Whenever any vacancy shall hereafter occur in the said office of Recorder of said City, the same shall be filled, for the unexpired portion of the official term, at the next annual City election thereafter, if sufficient time intervene to give the notice required by law: *Provided*, That if such time does not intervene, or if such vacancy occurs more than three months prior to the next ensuing annual City election after the happening of such vacancy, the Common Council may, in its discretion, order a special election to fill such vacancy for the residue of the official term.

CHAPTER 4.

CITY ATTORNEY.

[Chapter One of the Revised Ordinances of 1863]

SECTION 1. The City Attorney shall have the charge of, and conduct, all the law business of the Corporation, and of all the Boards, Officers, Departments, and Committees thereof, and all other law business in which the City shall be interested, when so ordered by the Common Council, and shall draw all leases, deeds, contracts and ordinances of the City.

SEC 2. He shall keep his office in such place as may be designated and provided by the City, and shall execute bonds to the Corporation in the amount of two thousand dollars.

SEC. 3. He shall, in writing, advise the Common Council, all Boards of the City, and their Officers and Committees, respectively, and the chief officer of any department or bureau of the City government, upon all matters which may be submitted to him for his opinion.

SEC. 4. He shall certify to the correctness of the form of all official bonds, deeds, leases and contracts of any kind, in which the City is interested, before the same shall be accepted or adopted by the Common Council, or any officer of the Corporation.

SEC. 5. He shall, when required by the Common Council, prepare the draft of any bill to be presented by the Corporation of the City to the Legislature for passage, with a proper memorial.

SEC. 6. He shall prosecute and defend all actions which may be brought by or against the Corporation or any board or officer thereof, when directed by the Common Council so to do. [*As amended by Ordinance approved October 20, 1870.*]

SEC. 7. He shall institute actions against all persons owing the Corporation for rents and licenses, or who may have incurred any penalty or forfeiture, under the Charter and Ordinances, or by reason of the breach of the condition of any official bond, when directed by the Common Council so to do. [*As amended by Ordinance approved October 20, 1870.*]

SEC. 8. He shall, once in every quarter, file a written statement, under oath, with the Controller, stating the nature and amount of any debt due to the Corporation, recovered by him, the person against whom, and the tribunal before which it was recovered, and the time when he recovered the same; and he shall, at the time of making said statement, pay all sums so recovered to the City Treasurer, who shall give him a voucher therefor, a copy of which he shall file with the Controller.

SEC. 9. He shall, on the first Tuesday in January, in each year, report to the Common Council, the titles and nature of all actions prosecuted or defended by him during the preceding year, and what actions are pending, what determined, and how, and such other information, concerning the law business of the City, as he deems proper.

SEC. 10. He shall keep in proper books, to be provided for the purpose, a register of all actions prosecuted or defended by him, and of all proceedings had therein; a list of all contracts, bonds, and other papers certified to by him, and copies of all opinions which he shall give upon any point submitted to him.

SEC. 11. He shall, at the expiration of every three months during his term of office, furnish the Controller with a sworn statement of all proper disbursements which he may have made in conducting the law business of the City, which amount shall be audited and allowed in the same manner as other accounts against the City. [*As amended by Ordinance approved October 20, 1870.*]

Sec. 12. He shall, when he deems it necessary, in the trial or argument of causes of importance, in which the City may be a party, or interested, request such additional counsel or aid as he may designate: *Provided*, That he shall, in all cases, inform the Common Council whom he wishes to employ, and shall employ no one without their consent.

Sec. 13. He shall, without special direction from the Common Council, institute all actions for rents, penalties, forfeitures, and license moneys, for all trespasses and injuries upon and to the property of the City, or any Board thereof.

Sec. 14. He shall examine all tax and assessment rolls before their confirmation, and make such alterations in the form thereof as may be necessary to their legality.

Sec. 15. All the principal officers of the City shall, from time to time, place in the hands of the Attorney, for his action, all claim for debt, money due, or damages done to the City, which may arise in or grow out of the office and business under their charge; and whenever suit is commenced against the Corporation, the officer on whom process is served shall deliver the same to him, and the said Attorney shall forthwith report the facts to the Council, and await instructions. [*As amended by Ordinance approved October 20, 1870.*]

CHAPTER 5.

CITY COUNSELOR.

[Chapter Two of the Revised Ordinances of 1863.]

Section 1. It shall be the duty of the Counselor to give to the Common Council, any Committee thereof, the Mayor, Controller, or any Board of the Corporation, when requested, his legal counsel and opinion on all legal questions arising under or concerning the

Charter or any Ordinance of the Corporation, and on all legal questions and subjects in which said Corporation shall be legally interested.

SEC. 2. The legal opinions of the Counselor shall be given in writing. When they are reported to the Common Council, they shall be printed and published as part of the proceedings of the meeting of said Council at which they are reported; and when they are reported to any Committee of such Council, to the Mayor or any Board of the Corporation, they shall be filed by such Committee, Mayor or Board in the office of the City Clerk.

SEC. 3. He shall appear as attorney and counsel in behalf of the Corporation in all suits, prosecutions or proceedings, which shall be brought in any Circuit Court, or in the Supreme Court of this State, or in any United States Court, by or against said Corporation, or any Board thereof, or which, when brought, shall be removed, in any mode whatever, from such Circuit Court, into the Supreme Court, and, as the case may require, shall prosecute or defend therein, to the termination thereof.

SEC. 4. He shall also, on the request of the Attorney, appear and act as his associate counsel in the Recorder's Court, in all suits, prosecutions or proceedings brought in said Court, by or against the Corporation, or any Board thereof, or brought under the provisions of the Chapter entitled "Chapter 7, opening, altering and closing streets;" and shall also, on the request of the Attorney, appear and act as his associate counsel in the Supreme Court, in all such suits, prosecutions or proceedings, when in any manner removed to such Supreme Court.

SEC. 5. He shall also, whenever directed by the Common Council, appear as attorney and counsel in behalf of any officer of the Corporation, in any suit, prosecution, or other judicial proceeding, brought by or against such officer, in his official character, and, as the case may require, shall prosecute and defend them, to the termination thereof.

SEC. 6. He shall not commence actions or other judicial proceedings, in behalf of the Corporation, or any Board thereof, except when so directed to do by the Common Council, or by such Board.

SEC. 7. He shall also act as a member of any Committee of the Common Council, and discharge the duties of a member thereof, whenever directed by said Council.

SEC. 8. He shall also prepare and report to the Common Council, upon their request, the draft of any bill to amend the Charter of the Corporation, or other bill, to be presented to the Legislature, together with a proper memorial to the Legislature, praying for its passage.

SEC. 9. He also shall examine and approve all leases, deeds and contracts, prepared by the City Attorney, to be entered into by the Corporation, or any Board thereof, or by any agent or officers, in behalf of such Corporation, or Board, and shall certify to the legal correctness, sufficiency and execution of the same.

SEC. 10. On the expiration of every quarter of his official term, he shall make a report, in writing, to the Controller, duly verified by his oath, of all sums of money received or collected by him during such quarter for and in behalf of the Corporation, and from whom and on what account or suit they were received or collected, and shall at the same time pay over the same to the Treasurer, who shall give duplicate vouchers thereof, one of which the Counselor shall file with the Controller. At the same time, he shall also make a report, in writing, to the Controller, duly verified by his oath, of all proper disbursements which he may have made in conducting the law business of the Corporation, and upon what account or suit, and how they were disbursed, and the same shall be audited and allowed as other accounts against the City. [*As amended by Ordinance approved October 20, 1870.*]

SEC. 11. He shall, on the first Tuesday in January of each year, make report in writing to the Common Council, duly verified by his oath, of all suits, prosecutions or actions prosecuted or defended by him during the preceding year; of the names of the parties thereto; of the titles of the Courts in which they were commenced; of their progress or final disposition; and when finally disposed of; the mode of their disposition, and all other information concerning the legal interests of the City, which he may deem necessary or proper.

SEC. 12. The Counselor shall be appointed by the Common

Council, on the nomination of the Mayor, and shall hold his office for the term of three years; he shall be a practicing attorney of the Supreme Court of this State, and of good standing as such; he shall keep an office in some public and convenient place in the City of Detroit, and shall, before entering on the duties of his office, give an official bond, duly conditioned: 1st, that he will not, while holding the office of Counselor for the City of Detroit, accept of any fee, retainer or reward of any kind from other parties for professional services to be rendered to them, except upon the express condition that such services shall not in any way conflict with his duties to the City as its Counselor; and, 2d, for the performance of all his duties as prescribed by the Charter and ordinances of the City. [*As amended by Ordinance approved October 20, 1870.*]

SEC. 13. He shall keep, in proper books, to be provided by the Corporation for the purpose, a register of all actions, prosecutions and proceedings, prosecuted or defended by him, and of the various doings therein; and on the expiration of his official term, he shall forthwith, on demand, deliver to his successor in office such register, together with all deeds, cases, contracts or other papers and writings in his possession, delivered to him by or belonging to the Corporation, any officer or Board thereof, or any Committee of the Common Council; and shall also deliver a written consent of substitution of his successor in all such actions, prosecutions or proceedings then pending and undetermined.

CHAPTER 6.

CITY TREASURER.

[Ordinance approved January 9th, 1866.]

SECTION 1. The City Treasurer shall give a bond, with two or more sufficient sureties, in such sum as the Common Council may, by resolution, from time to time determine; which bond shall be approved of and conditioned as is now or hereafter may be required by law, and which shall be deposited with the City Clerk.

SEC. 2. He shall, once in each week, report to the City Controller a statement in detail of the entire amount of his receipts from all sources, subsequent to the last item in his preceding statement, and also showing the sources from which, and the account on which, the same was received, and also the disbursements made by him during the week. The Controller shall thereupon examine said report, and report to the Council such facts in relation thereto as he may deem necessary, and shall transmit said report, with his approval or disapproval thereon, to said Common Council. [*As amended by Ordinance approved December 5, 1870.*]

SEC. 3. He shall deposit daily his entire receipts from all sources, and all money and checks on hand, to the credit of the City of Detroit, in such bank as may be designated by the Common Council as the depository of the funds of the city: *Provided, however,* That he may retain in his office, in currency, a sum not to exceed, at any time, one thousand dollars, to meet and pay coupons and small disbursements. He shall also deposit, in the same bank, all moneys, bonds and other securities held by the Commissioners of the Sinking Fund, which last shall be made special deposits and shall be inclosed in a sealed envelope, having indorsed thereon a memorandum of its contents, and which, so sealed and indorsed, shall be placed in a metal box with a secure lock, to be provided by the City, and marked "Detroit Sinking Fund." All such special deposits shall be made and held subject to the order of the Mayor and Treasurer of said City of Detroit. [*As amended by Ordinance approved January 27, 1866.*]

SEC. 4. He shall pay out no money except from the said sum authorized to be retained in his office for the purpose specified in Section 3, save by his check upon said bank, except his ordinary disbursements on pay rolls of city officers; and such check, to render it valid, shall have written or printed, or partly written and partly printed, upon the same paper therewith, a duplicate of the warrant of the Controller, authorizing or requiring the payment of the sum thereby drawn for. All warrants drawn by the Controller upon the Treasurer for the payment of money, shall be drawn and signed in duplicate, one of which shall have written or printed upon its face the word "original," which shall be kept and filed in his office by the Treasurer; and the other of which shall have written or printed on its face the word "duplicate," which last shall be and remain unsevered from the check of the Treasurer: *Provided, however, and it is expressly ordained,* That all moneys belonging to the "Board of Education of the City of Detroit," and to the "Detroit Metropolitan Police Fund," shall be drawn and paid out by said Treasurer in such mode and manner as shall be prescribed by said Board and the Board of Police Commissioners, in conformity with law. [*As amended by Ordinance approved January 27, 1866.*]

SEC. 5. It shall be the duty of the Committee on Ways and Means to examine, at least once in each month, the books, papers, vouchers, securities, deposits and disbursements of the said Treasurer, and in case they find any defalcation, discrepancy or irregularity in the same, to at once notify his bondsmen thereof, and also to report the same to the Council at the next session.

SEC. 6. Whenever the Controller shall draw his warrant for the payment of any bond or coupon, it shall be his duty to write across the face of such bond or coupon the word "warrant," and to affix thereafter his initials, so as to indicate that the same has been paid.

CHAPTER 7.

CITY ASSESSOR.

[Chapter Four of the Revised Ordinances of 1863.]

SECTION 1. The City Assessor shall be appointed by the Common Council, upon the recommendation of the Mayor, and shall hold his office for the term of three years, and shall devote his whole time to the service of the City in connection with the duties of his office.

SEC. 2. Before entering upon the duties of his office the Assessor shall take and subscribe the oath provided in the City Charter, and shall execute a bond to the Corporation with one or more sufficient sureties, conditioned that he will faithfully perform the duties of his office, and on demand deliver over to his successor or other proper officer or agent of the Corporation, all books, papers, moneys, effects and property belonging to the Corporation or appertaining to his office. [*As amended by Ordinance approved October 20, 1870.*]

SEC. 3. On the first day of October, in each year, the Assessor shall appoint two competent persons to act as Assistant Assessors, who shall hold their offices for such time as may be necessary, not exceeding six months, take and subscribe the oath herein provided for the Assessor; and in making assessments the Assessor and his assistants shall, as far as practicable, act conjointly. [*As amended by Ordinance approved November 24, 1865. See, also, Session Laws, 1867.*]

SEC. 4. The Assessor and his assistants shall, between the first days of October and April in each year, in the manner provided in the City Charter, assess all the real and personal property, subject to assessment or taxation within the several wards of the City, and within the same period shall make out and complete the assessment rolls for each ward, in proper books to be provided for that purpose. [*As amended by Ordinance approved November 24, 1865. See, also, Session Laws, 1867.*]

SEC. 5. The Assessor shall keep in his office complete sets of assessment rolls made by him and confirmed by the Common Council, and all books, rolls and records in his office, shall be open to public inspection at all convenient hours of the day.

SEC. 6. The Assessor may require the services of the City Surveyor in ascertaining the divisions and boundaries of any real estate within the City; and it is hereby made the duty of said Surveyor to render such services whenever applied to by the Assessor.

SEC. 7. The Assessor is hereby authorized to employ such clerical assistance as the business of his office may render necessary; and such clerical assistants shall, for the time they are actually employed, receive such compensation per diem as the Common Council shall, from time to time, fix by resolution. [*As amended Ordinance approved March 22, 1864.*]

Sec. 8. The Assessor shall have power to procure of the contractor for supplying stationery, books or printing for the City, such books, stationery and printing as he may, from time to time, require for his office, and the same shall be paid for by the City of Detroit.

Sec. 9. When required by the City Controller, the Assessor shall prepare the tax rolls for highway, sewer, school and City taxes of each ward in the City, and deliver the same, when completed, to the Controller; he shall also prepare the tax rolls for State and County taxes for each ward in the City, and deliver the same, when completed, to the County Treasurer.

Sec. 10. The Assessor shall carefully preserve and keep all books, papers and records, appertaining to or filed in his office.

Sec. 11. The Assessor shall, on the first Monday in each month, make out and file with the City Controller, a monthly roll, with his certificate attached thereto, giving the names of the Assistant Assessors and clerical assistants permanently employed in his office, and the time they were actually employed in their official duties. Upon the receipt of such roll with the certificate of the Assessor the Controllor shall transmit the same to the Council, as in other cases of accounts against the City. Temporary clerical assistants shall be paid for their services in the same manner upon presenting to the Controller the certificate of the Assessor setting forth the actual time such assistants have been employed. [*As amended by Ordinance approved October 20, 1870.*]

CHAPTER 8.

CITY COLLECTOR.

[Chapter Five of the Revised Ordinances of 1863.]

Section 1. Before entering upon the duties of his office the City Collector shall execute a bond to the City of Detroit, conditioned that he will faithfully perform the duties of his office, and will, on demand, or at the expiration of his term of office, deliver over to his successor in office, or other proper officer or agent of the Corporation, all books, papers, moneys, effects and property belonging to the Corporation, or appertaining to his office, which may be in his custody, as an officer, and that he will pay over to the Corporation, or its legally authorized agent, all money received by him, at the time and in the manner prescribed by the Charter and Ordinances of the City. [*As amended by Ordinance approved October 20, 1870.*]

SEC. 2. It shall be the duty of the City Collector to collect all special assessments imposed and levied by the Common Council, except such as shall be paid by the person assessed to the Receiver of Taxes, prior to the issue of the warrant for the collection of the same, as is, or may be provided by the Ordinances of the City.

SEC. 3. It shall be the duty of the City Collector, during the time he has any tax or assessment roll in his hands for collection of special assesment, in the City of Detroit, at least once in seven days, to deposit with the Receiver of Taxes, all sums of money collected by him during said seven days, and since his last deposit for which sums he shall take the Receiver's receipt, which he shall, within twenty-four hours after receiving the same, show to the Controller of the City, and shall at the time, file with the Controller a statement in writing, that the amount so deposited by him with said Receiver of Taxes, was all the money belonging to the Corporation of said City, collected by him, and in his possession at the time of making said deposit, which statement shall be signed by the Collector making the same, and sworn to by him, before the Controller, who shall report said statement to the Common Council, with his allowance or disallowance indorsed thereon, in the same manner as other accounts are audited and indorsed by him. But in case the City Collector shall not have collected any money during seven days, then he shall report the fact to the Receiver of Taxes, and shall make a sworn statement of the same to the Controller.

SEC. 4. It shall be the duty of the City Collector to collect from the persons named in the respective assessment rolls placed in his hands, the assessment of tax therein specified and set forth as due from such persons, and for such purpose he may levy upon and sell the personal property, subject to levy for such tax or assessment, of any person liable to pay, and refusing or neglecting to do so. The Collector may levy upon the property of the persons named in the warrant liable, wherever the same may be found in the City of Detroit. [*As amended by Ordinance approved December 12, 1870.*]

SEC. 5. Upon receiving the assessment roll, or a copy thereof, and warrant, it shall be the duty of the City Collector to proceed to demand and collect the several sums mentioned therein, and if any person shall neglect or refuse to pay the same, then, if he can find any goods or chattels of the person liable therefor, he shall levy thereon; but, before he shall proceed to sell such goods and chattels, he shall give ten days previous notice of the time and place of sale, by causing the same to be posted up in three of the most conspicuous places in said City, and the property levied upon shall be sold at public auction to the highest bidder; and the City Collector shall render the overplus, if any, after deducting the costs and charges of such distress and sale, to the person entitled thereto. The City Collector shall in all cases be entitled to demand and collect five cents on the dollar on the amount of the assessment, which the person so assessed shall pay, and which shall be deposited as other moneys received by said City Collector. [*As amended by Ordinance approved December 12, 1870.*]

SEC. 6. The City Collector shall make return of his doings within the time mentioned in said warrant to the Common Council, if in session; but if not, then at their next ensuing meeting, and in such return describe the goods and chattels sold, and the amount which each article sold for. But if goods and chattels cannot be found, or if such person or persons mentioned in said roll are non-residents of said City, the City Collector shall state such fact, verified by an affidavit taken before the City Controller, and annex the same to a list of such lands on which the assessments have not been paid.

CHAPTER 9.

WARD COLLECTORS.

[Chapters Six and Seven of the Revised Ordinances of 1863.]

SECTION. 1. The Collector of each Ward shall collect all State and County Taxes assessed and imposed upon the real and personal property of such Ward, and all such City, Highway, Sewer and School Taxes as shall be placed in his hands for collection by the Receiver of Taxes.

SEC. 2. The penalty of the bond of each Ward Collector, given to said City for the faithful performance of his duties, shall be in such sum as the Council shall direct. [*As amended by Ordinance approved December 5, 1870.*]

SEC. 3. It shall be the duty of each Collector, during the time he has any tax roll in his hands for collection of City Taxes, at least once in seven days, to deposit with the Receiver of Taxes all sums of money collected by him during said seven days, and since his last deposit, for which sums he shall take the Receiver's receipt; which he shall, within twenty-four hours after receiving the same, show to the Controller of the City, and shall at the time file with the Controller a statement, in writing, that the amount so deposited by him with said Receiver of Taxes was all the money belonging to the Corporation of said City, collected by him, and in his possession at the time of making said deposit, which statement shall be signed by the Collector making the same, and sworn to by him before the Controller, who shall report said statement to the Common Council, with his allowance or disallowance indorsed thereon in the same manner as other accounts audited and indorsed by him. But in case any Collector shall not have collected any money during seven days, then he shall report the fact to the Receiver of Taxes, and shall make a sworn statement of the same to the Controller.

SEC. 4. It shall be the duty of the Collectors to collect from the persons named in their respective assessment rolls, the assessment or tax therein specified and set forth as due from such persons; and for such purposes, they may levy upon and sell the personal property of any kind or description of any person liable to pay and refusing or neglecting to do so. And any Collector may levy upon the property of such person, wherever the same may be found in the City of Detroit.

SEC. 5. Any person or persons who shall resist, obstruct or hinder any City Collector or Ward Collector of said City in levying upon or taking into possession any goods and chattels under and by virtue of a warrant, legally issued and directed to said City Collector or Ward Collector, for the collection of any tax or assessment of said City—said goods and chattels being legally liable to be so levied on and taken into possession by said City Collector or Ward Collector—shall be punished by a fine not to exceed five hundred dollars, or by imprisonment not to exceed one year, or by both such fine and imprisonment, in the discretion of the Court.

SEC. 6. Any person who shall prevent any City Collector or Ward Collector from entering upon any house or premises occupied by him or her, for the purpose of searching for or levying on goods and chattels, under any warrant legally issued for the collection of tax or assessment, which the person so occupying said house or premises is liable to pay, shall be punished by the same fine or imprisonment, or by both, in the discretion of the Court, as is provided in the preceding section.

CHAPTER 10.

RECEIVER OF TAXES.

[Chapter Eight of the Revised Ordinances of 1863.]

SECTION 1. There shall be an officer in and for the City of Detroit to be denominated the Receiver of Taxes, with the powers and duties, in addition to those prescribed in the Charter, hereinafter prescribed, to be appointed by the Common Council, on the nomination of the Mayor, and to hold his office for two years, and receive such salary as the Common Council shall prescribe. [*As amended by Ordinance approved December 5, 1870.*

SEC. 2. Before entering upon the duties of his office, the Receiver of Taxes shall execute a bond to the City of Detroit, with two sureties, conditioned that he will faithfully perform the duties of his office, and will, on demand, or at the expiration of his term of office, deliver over to his successor in office, or other proper officer or agent of the Corporation, all books, papers, moneys, effects, and property belonging to the Corporation, or appertaining to his office, which may be in his custody as an officer, and that he will pay over to the Corporation, or its legally authorized agent, all money received by him.

SEC. 3. The Receiver of Taxes shall keep, in books to be provided for the purpose, just and accurate accounts of all moneys received by him, showing the amount of all moneys received and credited to the several funds of the City, and the amount paid over to the City Treasurer; and where money is received by him in payment of any special assessment, for the construction of lateral sewers, or for building of side and crosswalks, or for the paving, grading, graveling, or macadamizing any street, lane or alley, or for repairing or otherwise improving the same, he shall, at the time of receiving such money, note in the proper book the lot or lots upon which such assessments were paid, and also the block or blocks in which such lot or lots are situated. He shall, on

Monday in each week, report, under oath, in writing, to the City Controller, the amount of money received by him, the particular funds to which the same has been credited, and if any special assessments, as above provided, have been paid, the lot or lots upon which such assessments have been paid, and the block or the blocks in which such lots are situated, and the name of contractor for doing the work, to pay which such assessment was made, and the amount paid over to the City Treasurer, as hereinafter provided, since the date of his last report.

Sec. 4. The Receiver of Taxes shall, on Monday and Thursday, in each week, pay over to the City Treasurer all money received by him, and shall, on Monday of each week, render to the Treasurer, in triplicate, a statement, in writing, of the amount of money received by him since his last deposit, the funds to which the same was credited, and where special assessments have been received by him, he shall give the number of the lot upon which the same were paid, and the block in which such lot is situated, and take the Treasurer's receipt upon two of such statements, one of which shall be filed with the City Controller, with the report provided for in section three, who shall report the same to the Common Council, at its next session.

Sec. 5. The Receiver of Taxes shall keep his office in such place as may be provided by the Common Council, where he shall be found at such reasonable hours of the day as shall be prescribed by the Common Council.

Sec. 6. The books in the office of the Receiver of Taxes shall, at all times, be open for the inspection of the Mayor, Controller, and any member or Committee of the Common Council.

Sec. 7. When assistance is necessary for the proper dispatch of the business of his office, he shall apply to the Common Council for the same, and such assistant, when appointed, shall receive such compensation as the Common Council shall by resolution prescribe. [*As amended by Ordinance approved December 5, 1870.*]

CHAPTER 11.

CITY SURVEYOR.

[Chapter Nine of the Revised Ordinances of 1863.]

SECTION. 1. It shall be the duty of the City Surveyor, when so directed by the Common Council, to ascertain and establish the proper grade to any avenue, street, lane, alley or sidewalk within the limits of said City, and when required, to run out and stake off the same.

SEC. 2. It shall also be his duty to make all necessary surveys, and superintend the construction, enlargement, or alteration of all drains connecting with the main or lateral sewers of said City, and shall record the same in a book to be provided by said Common Council, and deposit the same with the City Clerk at the termination of his said office.

SEC. 3. He shall also make all necessary surveys, and give such information as may be needed by any Committee, or by the Superintendent of the Water Works, in laying down, extending or connecting the water logs or pipes of said water works in said City, and shall, at all times, when required, consult and act with any Standing or Special Committee, who may desire any information or assistance in any matter or thing connected with the duties of his office where the City of Detroit is concerned.

SEC. 4. He shall also deliver over to the City Clerk all papers, plans and drafts relating to any survey made by order of the Common Council, and shall also make a written report of his doings and proceedings in all cases, when required so to do by the Common Council.

CHAPTER 12.

STREET COMMISSIONERS.

[Chapter Ten of the Revised Ordinances of 1863.]

SECTION 1. Before entering upon the duties of their respective offices, the Street Commissioners shall take and subscribe the oath of office provided in the City Charter, and shall execute a bond to the Corporation, with two or more sureties, in such sum as the Common Council shall prescribe, conditioned that they will faithfully perform the duties of their respective offices, and, on demand, deliver to their successors in office or other proper officer or agent of the Corporation, all books, papers, property and effects in their hands belonging to the City of Detroit.

SEC. 2. The Street Commissioners shall keep their office in such places as shall be provided by the Common Council.

SEC. 3. The City of Detroit is hereby divided into two Street Commissioners' Districts, as follows: The third, fourth, sixth, seventh and tenth Wards shall constitute one district, to be called the "Eastern District," and the first, second, fifth, eighth and ninth Wards shall constitute a district, to be called the "Western District."

SEC. 4. The Street Commissioners, within their respective districts, under the direction of the Common Council, shall superintend the construction, repairs, and cleaning of pavements, sidewalks, crosswalks, culverts and bridges, and direct the working, cleaning and improving of the highways, streets, alleys and public places, in the City of Detroit.

SEC. 5. It shall be the duty of the Street Commissioners to keep an accurate record of the names of all persons employed by them in the several wards of their respective districts, together with the number of horses, carts, wagons or other vehicles employed by them, and the amount of compensation to be paid for the same.

Sec. 6. The Street Commissioners shall, on Monday of each week, during their terms of office, report, in writing, under oath, to the City Controller, the cost of all repairs upon streets, side and crosswalks, bridges and culverts in their respective districts, and also the number of persons, horses or other animals, carts, wagons and other vehicles employed by them in the several wards of their respective districts, since the date of their last reports, and the length of time each was employed, and also the amount to be paid for the same.

Sec. 7. All materials or goods of any kind, to be used by the Street Commissioners, shall be purchased by the City Controller, and all contracts for constructing bridges or culverts, or for repairing streets, crosswalks, bridges or culverts, shall be made by him, under the direction of the Common Council: *Provided, however*, That when the expenses of such supplies shall exceed the sum of two hundred dollars, the same shall be let to the lowest responsible bidder, as provided in the City Charter.

Sec. 8. The Commissioners shall, from time to time, report to the Common Council the condition of the side and crosswalks, streets, lanes, alleys and public spaces within their respective districts, and make such recommendations for the improvement of the same as they shall think for the best interest of the City.

Sec. 9. The Street Commissioners shall promptly report to the Mayor any negligence or dereliction of duty on the part of the Overseers of Highways in the discharge of their official duties. (*See Sec. 21, City Charter.*) They shall also make complaint to the City Attorney for all violations of the Ordinances of the City which may come under their observation, whose duty it shall be to file complaints for the same in the Recorder's Court.

CHAPTER 13.

BOARD OF SEWER COMMISSIONERS.

[Chapter Forty-six of the Revised Ordinances of 1863.]

SECTION 1. The Board of Sewer Commissioners shall, annually, dating from the time of their organization, elect one of their number President.

SEC. 2. The Engineer of Sewers shall act as Secretary of said Board, and shall, under the direction of said Board, superintend the construction and repairs of all public sewers or drains, and pools, and sewers and drains built by special assessments. His salary shall be fixed by resolution of the Common Council.

SEC. 3. Said Board, when specially authorized by resolution of the Common Council, may appoint such inspectors of work, and other agents, as may be required for carrying out the work committed to their charge, by the Charter and by this Ordinance, which inspectors and agents shall receive such compensation for their services as the Common Council may allow or prescribe.

SEC. 4. Said Board shall have the supervision of the construction of all sewers hereafter to be built, whether they be built at the expense of the City, or by special assessment upon the individuals to be benefited thereby, and of all repairs of sewers and pools hereafter to be performed, and are hereby fully authorized and empowered to enforce, or otherwise carry out all contracts for the building or repairing of sewers, drains and pools within said City.

SEC. 5. Said Board shall, as soon as may be, submit to the Common Council a plan for constructing sewers and drains for the whole City, having reference, however, to the sewers and drains already constructed, or in process of construction, and said Board shall have the control of all public sewers and private drains already constructed or in process of construction, as well, also, as all public and private sewers within the City, and shall in the month of March of each year report to said Common Council what public sewers and drains they deem necessary to build in that year, and shall accompany the report with an estimate of the cost of each and all of said sewers, and of all the probable expense of the construction of public sewers during the fiscal year ending January thereafter. [*As amended by Ordinance approved December 12, 1870.*]

SEC. 6. The Common Council shall decide which of the sewers so recommended by the Board shall be built in said year, and shall, through the City Clerk, notify said Board of their decision, and the Common Council shall not have power to build or contract to build any public sewer or sewers within said City that the Board of Sewer Commissioners has not recommended in their report in the month of March, and said Board shall, without delay, report to said Common Council an estimate of the cost of any public sewer or drain which the Common Council shall order to be built, and which was not embraced in the estimate provided for in the foregoing section, and shall proceed to advertise for proposals to build all the sewers and drains ordered to be built by the Common Council, under such specifications and forms as the said Board may deem necessary; which advertisement shall be published at least ten days in the newspaper published by the contractor to do the City printing, and shall state the time when and the place where said proposals shall be received and opened, and shall require each party making a proposal to accompany the same with a statement, in writing, signed by at least two persons, who agree thereby to become sureties in an amount at least double the estimated cost of the work proposed to be performed, for the faithful performance of the said work. [*As amended by Ordinance approved December 12, 1870.*]

SEC. 7. Said proposals shall be received and opened by said Board publicly, in the office of the City Controller, and in his presence, and a copy of each proposal shall be recorded by the said City Controller, and also by the Secretary of said Board.

SEC. 8. When said proposals shall have been received and opened, as aforesaid, said Board, together with the City Controller, shall proceed to examine the same, and determine who are the lowest responsible bidders, possessing the qualifications required by the Charter of said City, whereupon the Controller shall communicate their determination, together with all said proposals, to the Common Council, who shall consider said proposals and communication, and award the contract proposed to be performed to the lowest responsible qualified bidder, and shall return said proposals, and communicate their decision to said Board. The said Board shall transmit the proper specifications of the work to be performed to the City Attorney, who shall draw a contract for the performance of said work in accordance with said specifications, and of the Charter and Ordinances of said City, which said contract shall be signed, on the part of the City, by said Board, and attested under the corporate seal by the City Clerk, and shall, when executed, be placed in the keeping of said Board, whose duty it shall be to see that the contractor, or contractors, shall comply therewith.

SEC. 9. Said Board shall certify to the amount due upon all contracts, and for all materials furnished, and labor performed, in building or repairing sewers or pools; and all bills and accounts thus certified, for amounts so due, shall be audited by the Controller, and presented by him to the Council, in the same manner as other bills and accounts against said City.

SEC. 10. Said Board shall keep, or cause to be kept, an accurate record of all their proceedings, which shall, at all times, be subject to the examination and inspection of any citizen of said City, and shall, once in each year, or oftener, if required, submit to said Common Council a report of all their proceedings, with the names of their employes, and the total expenses of the construction and repairs of sewers and pools, since the last report, and such other information as they may deem necessary, or as said Council may require.

SEC. 11. Said Board shall not lay down or construct any sewer or pool in said City, or purchase any materials, or enter into any contract, except as provided in this Ordinance, and except in case of any unexpected casualty or damage to the sewers or pools of said City, in which case said Board may cause the same to be repaired, to the amount of not exceeding two hundred dollars, and shall report their proceedings therein, and the necessity therefor, to the next regular meeting of the Common Council.

SEC. 12. No connection shall be made with any public sewer or drain, except with the permission of said Board, and under the direction of the Engineer, who shall, at least once in each month, notify the City Assessor of all such connections, made since the last notice; and any person connecting with any public sewer, without such permission, shall be fined not to exceed one hundred dollars, or imprisoned three months, or both, in the discretion of the Court.

SEC. 13. The City Clerk shall supply the said Board with all necessary stationery.

CHAPTER 14.

COMMISSIONERS OF GRADES.

[Ordinance approved July 12, 1869.]

SECTION. 1. That there shall be three Commissioners of Grades in and for the City of Detroit, who shall be appointed, on nomination of the Mayor, by the Common Council of said City, and who shall serve without compensation, and shall continue in office until removed by said Council.

SEC. 2. The said Commissioners of Grades and City Surveyor shall have power to fix, alter and establish the grades upon all streets, alleys and public spaces in said City, preparatory to the paving, grading, graveling, planking, macadamizing, or otherwise working the same, and the laying of side and crosswalks thereon; to establish permanent measurements or bench marks whenever necessary; to keep a record of the grades established, and to report said grades for confirmation by the Council.

SEC. 3. Whenever any grade, reported to the Common Council aforesaid, shall be confirmed, it shall be recorded in the Grade Book of said City, and shall be, and continue the grade of the street, sidewalk, alley, or public space for which it was intended.

CHAPTER 15.

OVERSEERS OF HIGHWAYS.

[Ordinance approved February 8, 1868.]

SECTION 1. The Overseer of Highways in each Ward shall receive a salary in lieu of all other compensation, to be fixed each year by the Common Council, and be paid out of the District Road Fund of the Ward from which he was elected.

SEC. 2. All horses and wagons or other vehicles used by such Overseer in the performance of his duties shall be hired by the Street Commissioner of the District to which he belongs, and none other than such as are hired by said Commissioner, shall be paid for by the City; nor shall either of the Street Commissioners, or any of the Overseers of Highways, be the owner of any horses, wagons, or other vehicle, employed by them, nor shall they, or any of them, be interested in the same, directly or indirectly.

SEC. 3. This Ordinance shall take effect when the compensation of Overseers of Highways, as mentioned in section one, shall be fixed.

[Ordinance Approved November 29, 1869.]

SEC. 4. Whenever any labor is performed upon any of the streets, highways, lanes, alleys or public spaces in the City of Detroit, under the supervision of the Overseers of Highways, it shall be the duty of said Overseers of Highways of each Ward to present to the Street Commissioner of the proper district the proper pay-roll therefor, with an affidavit of said Overseer indorsed on the back thereof, stating that the persons named in said pay-roll actually performed the work as therein charged; that the time mentioned therein was actually and necessarily employed in the performance of said work; that said labor was performed exclusively for the benefit of the Corporation of the City of Detroit, and that the amount stated in said pay-roll for said work, is just, true and correct. And each Overseer shall preserve in his office a duplicate of each pay-roll presented, with the duplicate number and copy of the affidavit indorsed thereon. Upon the receipt of said pay-roll by the Street Commissioner, he shall transmit the same to the Controller, duly certified, under his signature.

SEC. 5. When the Controller shall have issued his warrant upon the City Treasurer for the payment of the amount due in said pay-rolls, it shall be the duty of said Overseer of Highways, within six days thereafter, to give the person entitled thereto an order upon the City Treasurer, from a book to be provided for that purpose, and to be kept in his, said Overseer's, office, which said order shall contain the number of the pay-roll, the district in which the work was performed, the number of days actually employed, the rate *per diem*, the amount due, and the person to whom the compensation is to be paid, as per pay-roll. The Overseer shall retain in said book in his office, for public inspection, a duplicate copy or stub of each order issued. Upon the presentation of said order to the City Treasurer, that officer shall pay to the person named in said pay-roll, and to no other, the amount stated in said pay-roll and order to be due.

SEC. 6. Any failure to comply with the provisions of this Ordinance shall be punished by a fine not exceeding one hundred dollars and costs, and in the imposition of such fine and costs, the court may make a further sentence that the offender be imprisoned in the Detroit House of Correction until the payment of such fine and costs: *Provided, however,* that such imprisonment shall not exceed the period of three months.

CHAPTER 16.

CITY PHYSICIANS.

[Chapter Eleven of the Revised Ordinances of 1863.]

SECTION 1. There shall be appointed by the Common Council, on the second Tuesday of January of each year, four Physicians, to be called "City Physicians," and who shall be of good standing in their profession, and shall possess and exercise the powers and duties hereafter prescribed.

SEC. 2. Before entering upon the duties of their respective offices, the City Physicians shall each take and subscribe the oath of office provided for in the City Charter.

SEC. 3. The City of Detroit is hereby subdivided into four districts, to be called "City Physician Districts," as follows: All that portion of the City of Detroit lying east of the centre of Woodward avenue, and south of Monroe avenue, and south of the centre of Clinton street, shall constitute and be known as City Physician District No. 1.

All that portion of the City of Detroit east of the centre of Woodward avenue, and north of and including Monroe avenue, and north of the centre of Clinton street, shall constitute and be known as City Physician District No. 2.

All that portion of the City of Detroit lying west of the centre of Woodward avenue, and south of Michigan avenue, shall constitute and be known as City Physician District No. 3.

All that portion of the City of Detroit lying west of the centre of Woodward avenue, and north of Michigan avenue, and including Michigan avenue, shall constitute and be known as City Physician District No. 4.

SEC. 4. The City Physicians, when required by the Common Council, or Board of Health, shall examine in their several districts, into all sources of danger to the public health, and shall, from time to time, make such recommendation to the Common

Council concerning the sanitary condition of the City as to them shall seem necessary and proper.

Sec. 5. It shall be the duty of the City Physicians, in their several districts, when directed by the Mayor, an Alderman, or Director of the Poor, to attend any sick, disabled or infirm person who may be a charge upon the City, and render such medical assistance as may be necessary—also, when any person is taken to the pest house, the physician of the district from which the patient is taken shall attend on the person so taken to the pest house.

Sec. 6. It shall be the duty of the City Physicians, in their several districts, to vaccinate, without charge, any inhabitant of the City of Detroit, not previously vaccinated, who may apply to them for that purpose; they shall also give certificates of vaccination to such children as may have been vaccinated by them.

Sec. 7. The City Physicians shall furnish, at their own expense, all medicines which may be necessary in the skillful and proper treatment of such sick or disabled persons as may be a charge upon the City, and also such vaccine matter as may be required to carry into force the provisions of section six of this Ordinance. But each City Physician shall be entitled, at the end of each quarter during his term of office, upon his affidavit, that he has vaccinated, free of charge, all inhabitants of the City of Detroit who have called upon him for that purpose, to receive from the City Treasury the sum of twelve dollars and fifty cents, in addition to the salary of his office.

Sec. 8. It shall be the duty of the City Clerk to procure, at the expense of the City, suitable cards, upon which shall be printed a copy of section six of this Ordinance, and also the names and residences of the City Physicians; such cards shall be placed and kept in conspicuous positions in the office of each City Physician, and in the offices of the Receiver of Taxes, the City Clerk, and Director of the Poor.

Sec. 9. No person shall be eligible to the office of City Physician who has not received a diploma from a respectable Medical College.

Sec. 10. All complaints against the City Physicians shall be made to the Mayor, who shall investigate the same, and, if necessary, report the case to the Common Council, with his opinion thereon.

SEC. 11. In case of the absence or inability, from any cause, of a City Physician to attend to the duties of the office, he shall, with the consent of the Mayor, provide a competent physician to fill his place.

CHAPTER 17.

CITY HISTORIOGRAPHER.

[Chapter Twelve of Revised Ordinances of 1863.]

SECTION 1. There shall be appointed by the Common Council an officer to be called the Historiographer, who shall hold his office during the pleasure of the Council.

SEC. 2. It shall be duty of the Historiographer to collect together, receive and safely keep all such books, papers, documents, and other matters, connected with, and illustrating the history of the City of Detroit, as he may be able to procure without expense to the City.

SEC. 3. It shall be the duty of the Historiographer to report, annually (and at such other time as he shall be required to do), to the Common Council, the state and condition of his department.

SEC. 4. The Historiographer shall, at any time when required by the Council, deliver over to such persons as the Council may direct, all books, papers and documents, and other things that may at any time come into his possession as such officer, and in default thereof he shall be liable to a penalty of one hundred dollars.

SEC. 5. The office of Historiographer being honorary, no compensation shall be allowed to said officer.

CHAPTER 18.

DIRECTOR OF THE POOR.

[Ordinance approved May 8, 1870.]

SECTION 1. Before entering upon the duties of his office, the Director of the Poor shall execute a bond to the City of Detroit, in such sum as shall be fixed by Ordinance, and with sufficient sureties, conditioned as prescribed by the Charter of the City of Detroit, and shall also subscribe the oath of office as therein prescribed.

SEC. 2. The Director of the Poor shall keep his office in such place as shall be provided by the Common Council, and shall keep the same open from 8 until 11 o'clock A. M., and from 2 until 5 o'clock P. M., each day, Sundays excepted, during the months of November, December, January, February, March, and April, and from 7½ until 11 o'clock A. M., and from 3 until 6 o'clock P. M., during the months of May, June, July, August, September and October.

SEC. 3. It shall be the duty of the Director of the Poor, when any person, being a city pauper, shall, by himself or another, apply to him for relief, to make immediate personal inquiry into the state and circumstances of the applicant, and if it shall appear that he or she is in such indigent circumstances as to require permanent support, and is not so sick, diseased, lame, or otherwise disabled as that he or she cannot safely or conveniently be removed, to remove such person to the County Poor House, to be relieved and cared for as his or her necessities may require; but if such person cannot be safely or conveniently removed, for any of the reasons hereinbefore specified, the Director of the Poor may afford such persons relief under the provisions of this Ordinance, until such time as he or she can be safely removed to the County Poor House. And if it shall appear that any person applying for relief, as aforesaid, requires only temporary or partial support, he shall afford him or her such relief as the circumstances of the case may require. Whenever, from sickness or other disability, the Director of the Poor shall deem it necessary and proper to place any city pauper in a hospital, he shall do so by removing such pauper to any proper hospital belonging to the City of Detroit, or to any hospital with which the City has a contract, and the board and care of such pauper shall be paid for in the same manner as other claims and demands against the Corporation.

SEC. 4. The Director of the Poor shall, on or before the first Monday in July in each and every year, report to the Common Council the quantity of wood which will, in his estimation, be required for the relief of the poor during the ensuing year.

SEC. 5. It shall be the duty of the Director of the Poor, when in his judgment it is proper, to grant charitable relief to any person, to give such person an order on some reputable dealer in the kind of article or articles thus required to be furnished, which said order shall be made payable only to the person to whom originally granted; and in no case shall such order include spirituous liquors.

SEC. 6. The Common Council shall, from time to time, upon the report of the Controller, that an appropriation is necessary for that purpose, appropriate out of the Poor Fund, limited sums, to be subject to the warrant of the Controller, to meet the approved expenditures of the Director of the Poor.

SEC. 7. It shall be the duty of the contractor furnishing wood to the Corporation to present to the Controller, on the first Monday in each month, a monthly account of wood furnished by him, together with all orders which shall have been drawn upon him by the Director of the Poor, which account shall be accompanied by an affidavit, as required by the City Charter, and shall be audited and allowed like other claims and demands against the Corporation, and paid out of the Poor Fund.

SEC. 8. It shall be the duty of the Director of the Poor to give to paupers needing medical aid an order therefor on the City Physician in whose district such pauper resides.

SEC. 9. It shall be the duty of the Controller to procure railroad tickets for paupers who may wish permanently to leave the State, when recommended so to do by the Director of the Poor.

SEC. 10. Whenever any sum or sums of money are appropriated by the Common Council for the use of the poor of said City, and the Controller shall have drawn his warrant for such appropriation, such money shall then be deposited to the credit of the Poor Fund, in the office of the City Treasurer, and at no other place; and whenever any contributions in money shall be received by the Director of the Poor, for the benefit of the poor of said City, upon the receipt thereof, said Director shall deposit such money in the office of the City Treasurer, and take his receipt therefor; and all orders issued by the said Director of the Poor, for the relief of the poor of said City, shall be payable at the City Treasurer's office, and at no other place. And upon presentation to the City Treasurer of orders issued by the Director of the Poor for the benefit of the poor of said City, said Treasurer shall pay the amount therein stated to the person or persons in said order named.

SEC. 11. It shall be the duty of the Director of the Poor to keep on record in his office the names of all persons receiving or having received charitable aid through him; which said sums shall be entered in books, one for each ward of the City, and the same having alphabetical references, and to be entered in such a manner as to be easy of access. Said books shall show, in legible form, the amount of aid which has been granted to such person, either in provisions, wood, medical attendance, or otherwise, and they shall also show the actual residence or habitation of such person in each Ward. Said books shall, during the office hours, as herein prescribed, be open for inspection by any person desiring to examine the same.

SEC. 12. It shall be the duty of the Director of the Poor of said City, in making out his monthly reports to the Common Council, to set forth in detail in said report the date of furnishing relief, the number of the order issued by him, the name of the person relieved, the number in the family, the number of the house, name of the street in which the applicant resides, the kinds of relief furnished, and the person or persons on whom drawn, and placing the names of all persons residing in the several Wards in the proper list for such Ward; and he shall also enter in a separate book, to be provided for that purpose, and to be kept in his office for public inspection, the amount of money and the value, as near as he can ascertain, of all contributions received by him for the poor of the City, with a particular description, and the date of each contribution, together with the name or names of the persons contributing for the purposes aforesaid, where the donors have no objections to their names appearing, and he shall, also, in said book, enter the names and places of residence of all persons to whom relief is afforded from such contributions, together with the nature and amount of the relief furnished in each case; and on or before the tenth day of each month, in connection with the City Controller, the Director of the Poor and the City Treasurer shall compare all orders issued by said Director and paid by said Treasurer, with said report and contribution book, and the said Controller shall thereupon cause to be canceled, on the face of said report and contribution book, each order returned and paid, and found by him to compare with the amount set forth in said report; and the Director of the Poor shall receive no contributions from any citizen or citizens or other person or persons to be disposed of by him in any manner contrary to the provisions of this Ordinance as herein stated.

Sec. 13. If any owner, captain or master of a vessel, or other person or persons, shall, by land or water, bring and leave within the limits of the City any person or persons, poor and unable to maintain themselves, they shall forthwith, or as soon as may be thereafter, transport the same back to the place whence they were taken, and shall provide all the necessary means of comfort and subsistence for such paupers, if requested by them, or by any citizen, until so transported. In case of refusal or neglect to provide for such paupers the necessary means of comfort and subsistence, as herein required, and any member of the Common Council, or Director of the Poor, shall make such provision, the same may be recovered back, and may form part of the judgment in a prosecution for a violation of this chapter.

Sec. 14. The Director of the Poor for said City shall have and exercise the same powers and duties, and shall be subject to the same liabilities and restrictions as the laws of this State prescribe relative to Directors of the Poor in any township of this State; and the laws of this State relative to township and county paupers shall be observed with respect to such paupers in said City, and all suits and prosecutions for violations of such laws may be brought in the Recorder's Court of said City.

SEC. 15. It shall be the duty of the Director of the Poor, within ten days after having completed his monthly report, as herein required, to furnish to the City Clerk lists of persons who have received aid through his office, as shown by the books thereof, arranged and denominated by Wards, and showing the residence or habitation of such persons in their respective Wards; and it shall then be the duty of the City Clerk to cause said names, arranged as herein provided, to be printed, and placed by him at the disposal of the respective Aldermen of the several Wards, to the extent of not to exceed one hundred copies in the aggregate.

SEC. 16. Any failure to comply with the provisions of this Ordinance shall be punished by a fine not to exceed one hundred dollars and costs, and in the imposition of such fine and costs the Court may make a further sentence that the offender be imprisoned in the Detroit House of Correction until the payment of such fine and costs: *Provided, however,* that such imprisonment shall not exceed the period of three months.

CHAPTER 19.

CLERK OF THE MARKET.

[Chapter Fourteen of the Revised Ordinances of 1863.]

SECTION 1. The Clerk of the Market shall be appointed by the Common Council on the second Tuesday in January of each year, and shall possess and exercise the powers and duties hereinafter prescribed.

SEC. 2. He shall have charge of the City Hall Market, take care of the buildings thereof; attend therein daily during market hours; keep the same in a clean and orderly condition; collect all rents of stalls and stands, and such fees from wagons, carts and other vehicles as may be fixed by the Common Council; see that market wagons and other vehicles occupy such positions so as not to interfere with public travel, as may be prescribed by the Common Council; carefully observe that the rules and regulations of the market are properly observed and respected, and make complaint for any infractions of such rules and regulations or of any Ordinances of the City. [*As amended by Ordinance approved December 12, 1870.*]

SEC. 3. He shall examine all articles offered and provisions exposed for sale in the market, and see that the same is of good and wholesome quality.

SEC. 4. He shall promptly report to the Controller the names of all persons renting stalls and stands in the market who are in arrears for rent; and immediately after their collection he shall pay into the City Treasury all money received for the rent of stalls and stands, or for fees received from wagons and other vehicles; he shall, on Saturday of each week, make a report under oath, in writing, to the Controller, in which he shall give the amount of money received by him for rent of stalls and stands, or for fees, of whom received, and when paid into the City Treasury. On the first Monday in each month he shall report, in writing, under oath, to the Controller, the names of all persons renting and occupying stalls or stands in the market, the time for which such stalls or stands are leased or rented, and the amount for which each of such stalls is rented.

SEC. 5. It shall be the duty of the Clerk of the Market to visit, from time to time, the several meat markets in the City, and see that the same are licensed as provided by law, and that all the provisions of the Ordinance relative to private meat markets are properly enforced. He shall make complaint for any infractions of the provisions of that Ordinance.

SEC. 6. Any neglect or refusal of the Clerk of the Market to comply with any duty imposed upon him by law, shall be cause for his removal from the office by the Mayor or Common Council.

CHAPTER 20.

WEIGHMASTERS.

[Chapter Fifteen of the Revised Ordinances of 1863.]

SECTION 1. There shall be two or more officers in and for the City of Detroit, to be denominated Weighmasters, to be appointed by the Common Council on the second Tuesday in January of each year, and shall hold their offices for one year, or until their successors are appointed, and possess and exercise the powers and duties hereinafter provided.

SEC. 2. The Weighmasters before entering upon the duties of their respective offices, shall each execute a bond to the City of Detroit, with one or more sureties, conditioned as prescribed in the City Charter, and shall also subscribe the oath of office prescribed therein.

SEC. 3. It shall be the duty of the Weighmasters to weigh any load of hay, coal or straw which may be brought to the public scales under their charge, and after deducting the weight of the cart, wagon or sled, they shall deliver to the owner a certificate specifying the weight. They shall receive for their services one cent and a half per hundred weight upon each and every load they shall weigh, not including, however, the deduction made as above provided. [*As amended by Ordinance approved January 6, 1871.*]

SEC. 4. Persons owning or having in charge carts, wagons or sleds, loaded with hay or straw, shall not permit the same to stand in any street, avenue, alley or public space; but all such carts, wagons or sleds, shall stand at, or adjoining the public hay scales, in such order as shall be prescribed by the Weighmaster. No person or persons shall sell or offer for sale any hay in said City by the cart, wagon or sled load, unless the same has been weighed by one of the Weighmasters of said City, as provided by this Ordinance.

SEC. 5. This Ordinance shall not apply to straw made up into and sold by the bundle.

SEC. 6. The Weighmasters shall designate the places in the public wood yards where animals may be exposed for sale, and all persons owning, or having animals in charge, shall strictly comply with the rules and regulations prescribed by the Weighmasters, for the good order and government of their respective yards.

SEC. 7. The Weighmaster shall be entitled to demand and receive from the owner, or person for whom he weighs any horse or neat cattle, the sum of ten cents per head; and for any sheep or hogs the sum of five cents per head. [*As amended by Ordinance approved December 12, 1870.*]

SEC. 8. The Weighmaster of the Eastern District shall pay into the City Treasury for the use of the hay scales in said District, one hundred and fifty dollars per annum. The Weighmaster of the Western District shall pay into the City Treasury for the use of the hay scales in said District, one hundred and fifty dollars per annum; the said sums to be paid quarterly.

SEC. 9. No person offering or exhibiting for sale a cow having a sucking calf, shall muzzle, or in any way prevent the calf from taking its natural nutriment from its mother.

SEC. 10. Any Weighmaster who shall be guilty of taking or demanding more compensation for his services than is prescribed by this Ordinance, or who shall be guilty of any fraud or peculation in his office, shall, in addition to the punishment hereinafter prescribed, be removed from office by the Mayor or Common Council.

SEC. 11. Any violation of, or failure to comply with the provisions of this Ordinance, shall be punished by a fine not to exceed one hundred dollars and costs; and in the imposition of any such fine and costs, the Court may make a further sentence, that the offender shall be committed to the County Jail, or Detroit House of Correction, until the same be paid, for any period of time not exceeding six months.

CHAPTER 21.

SEALER OF WEIGHTS AND MEASURES.

[Ordinance Approved April 25, 1870.]

SECTION 1. There shall be in and for the City of Detroit an officer to be denominated the Sealer of Weights and Measures, who shall be appointed by the Board of Police from the members of the Metropolitan Police Force; and the person so appointed shall have the exclusive power to perform all the duties pertaining to his office, and shall, during the time he is directed by said Board to perform said duties, try and prove all scales, beams, weights and measures used in said City for the purpose of buying and selling, and such as shall be found conformable to the standards kept in his office, he shall stamp with the word "approved," or the letter "M," and the year in which said inspection is made; and such as are found not to be conformable to the standard in his office, he shall stamp with the word "condemned," and the year in which the inspection is made.

SEC. 2. The Sealer of Weights and Measures shall be provided by the City of Detroit with a book, to be kept in his office, in which he shall register, in alphabetical order, the name of each person whose weights, measures, scales, beams, or other instruments he has inspected; the number and size of the same, and what number of each was approved and condemned, with the time of inspection; and such book shall at all reasonable times be open to the inspection and examination of the public.

SEC. 3. It shall also be the duty of the said Sealer of Weights and Measures once in each year, and oftener if he deems it necessary, to inspect all wood boxes or measures used by wood dealers in said City, from which is sold or offered for sale or delivered sawed or sawed and split wood by the cord, half cord or less quantities; and all such boxes or measures found conformable to the standard (which standard shall not be less than one hundred and fifty cubic feet for a cord, and not less than seventy-five cubic feet for a half cord) to be kept in his office, he shall stamp with the word "approved," and the year in which each inspection is made; and all such boxes or measures found not conformable to the standard in his office he shall stamp with the word "condemned," and the year in which such inspection is made.

SEC. 4. No person shall neglect or refuse to exhibit any weights, measures, scales, beams, or other instruments used by him or her, in weighing or measuring, or any box or measure from which is sold or offered for sale, or delivered, any sawed, or sawed and split wood in any quantity, to the Sealer of Weights and Measures, when demanded by him, for the purpose of having the same inspected.

SEC. 5. No person shall use, for buying or selling, any weights, measures, scales, beams, or other instruments, or for buying or selling or delivering sawed, or sawed and split wood in any quantity, any box or measure, unless the same has been inspected and stamped "approved," or with the letter "M" by the Sealer of Weights and Measures. And all boxes or measures from which sawed, or sawed and split wood is sold, offered for sale or delivered, shall be bound by an iron band running around the upper edge of said boxes or measures.

SEC. 6. Any person who shall neglect or refuse to exhibit his weights, measure, scales, beams or other instruments used for the purpose of weighing or measuring, to the Sealer of Weights and Measures; or neglect or refuse to exhibit to said Sealer of Weights and Measures, when demanded by him, any box or measure used for the purchase, sale or delivering of sawed or sawed and split wood as above provided, for the purpose of having the same inspected, as hereinbefore provided; or who shall use, in buying or selling, any weights, measures, scales, beams, or other instruments used for weighing or measuring, or shall use for the purpose of buying, selling or delivering wood, as aforesaid, any box or measure which shall have been inspected and condemned by the Sealer of Weights and Measures, or which, not having been inspected and approved, shall not be conformable to the standards provided by law, shall be punished by a fine not to exceed one hundred dollars and costs of prosecution ; and the Court may make a further sentence, that the offender be imprisoned in the Detroit House of Correction till the payment of such fine and costs: *Provided,* That such imprisonment shall not exceed the period of six months.

CHAPTER 22.

INSPECTOR OF GAS METERS.

[Chapter Seventeen of the Revised Ordinances of 1863.]

SECTION 1. There shall be an officer in the City of Detroit, to be denominated "The Inspector of Gas Meters," with the powers and duties hereinafter prescribed, to be appointed by the Common Council, and to hold his office for one year, or until his successor is appointed.

SEC. 2. The Inspector of Gas Meters shall receive a salary of $1,000 per annum, $600 to be paid by the Detroit Gas Company, and $400 by the City of Detroit, in equal monthly payments. [*As amended by Ordinance approved September 7, 1870.*]

SEC. 3. Before entering upon the duties of his office, the Inspector of Gas Meters shall execute a bond to the City of Detroit, with two sureties, conditioned as provided in the City Charter, and shall also subscribe the oath therein prescribed. The bond and oath shall be filed in the office of the City Clerk.

SEC. 4. He shall keep his office in a room to be provided by the Common Council, where he shall be found at all convenient hours of the day.

SEC. 5. He shall keep in his office a good and accurate standard photometer, meter and prover, to be furnished by the City of Detroit.

SEC. 6. Whenever requested, he shall examine and test, without charge, any meter furnished by the Gas Company, which may be brought to his office, and shall give notice to the consumer and the Gas Company of the time when any meter is to be examined and tested; and after testing and proving any meter, he shall duly stamp the same.

SEC. 7. His inspection shall be conclusive upon both the Gas Company and the consumer, as to the accuracy of any meter; and whenever any meter shall be found to be imperfect or inaccurate, it shall be replaced by the Gas Company with a good and sufficient one.

SEC. 8. It is hereby made the duty of the Inspector of Gas Meters to keep a supervision over the public lamps of the City, and see that they are kept clean and in good order, and at all times provided with good and sufficient burners, of equal size. He shall, at the end of each month, examine the public meters, and make a record of the number of feet of gas indicated by such meters, and shall compare the same with the bill of gas presented to the City by the Gas Company. [*As amended by Ordinance approved September 7, 1870.*]

SEC. 9. The Inspector of Gas Meters shall, from time to time, make photometrical tests of the gas furnished by the Gas Company, and shall communicate to the Common Council the result of such tests.

SEC. 10. He shall, from time to time, give the Council information of the condition of the public lamps of the City, and of the quality of the gas furnished by the Gas Company.

SEC. 11. He shall keep a book in his office, in which he shall record the number of each meter, and the time when it was tested and proved by him, and such record shall be open at all times for public inspection.

SEC. 12. He may be suspended at any time by the Mayor, without charges, who shall report the same to the Common Council.

CHAPTER 23.

INSPECTORS OF FIREWOOD.

[Ordinance approved November 29, 1869.]

SECTION 1. There shall be four officers in and for the City of Detroit to be denominated Inspectors of Firewood, to be appointed by the Common Council, and to hold office for one year, or until their successors are appointed, and who shall possess and exercise the powers and duties hereinafter provided.

SEC. 2. The City of Detroit is hereby divided by Woodward avenue and Fort street into four wood inspection districts, to be known as the Eastern, Western, Northern and Southern Districts. To each of said districts there shall be appointed one of the aforesaid Inspectors.

SEC. 3. The Inspectors, before entering upon the duties of their respective offices, shall execute a bond to the City of Detroit, with one or more sureties, and conditioned as prescribed in the Charter of the City of Detroit, and shall also subscribe the oath therein.

SEC. 4. The Inspectors for the Northern and Southern Districts shall keep their respective offices at or near the public wood-yards, and shall keep the same open each day, Sunday excepted, between the hours of 7 o'clock A. M. and 6 o'clock P. M. They shall have charge of the wood yards in their respective districts, and all persons using such yards shall conform to the rules and regulations prescribed by the Inspector.

SEC. 5. The Inspectors for the Eastern and Western Districts shall keep their respective offices in some convenient place near the dock, and the same shall be open each day, Sunday excepted, between the hours of 7 A. M and 6 o'clock P. M.

SEC. 6. The Inspectors of the Northern and Southern Districts shall measure all wood which may be sold or offered for sale in the public wood-yards, and they shall receive for their services the following compensation, and no more: For measuring a load drawn by one horse or other animal, five cents; for measuring a load drawn by two or more horses or other animals, ten cents.

SEC. 7. No person shall sell or offer to sell wood by the wagon, cart or sled load, unless the same has been measured by the Wood Inspector at one of the wood-yards, nor shall such wood be kept for sale in any place in said city except at one of the public wood yards.

SEC. 8. No person owning or having in charge any wagon, cart or sled, containing wood for sale, shall permit the same to stand in any street, alley or public space.

SEC. 9. The Inspectors for the Eastern and Western Districts shall measure all wood which may be brought to the City in boats, or other watercraft, for the purpose of being sold. They shall receive for their services the following compensation, and no more. For measuring ten cords or under, ten cents per cord, and five cents for each additional cord.

SEC. 10. Persons bringing wood to this City in boats or other craft, for the purpose of selling the same, shall, before selling the same, cause it to be measured by the Wood Inspector of the district, and if necessary to the more accurate measurement of the same, they shall cause it to be piled in a convenient place on the wharf or dock.

SEC. 11. On the receipt of their legal compensation, the several Wood Inspectors, shall deliver to the person employing them, a certificate, stating the number of feet contained in the wagon, cart or sled load measured by them; or the number of cords, or parts of a cord, contained in any boat or water craft, or pile measured by them; and in making their measurement, they shall examine carefully the manner in which the wood is piled in the vehicle, boat, craft or pile, and make a reasonable and fair deduction for improper or unfair piling, or for the crookedness or unevenness of the wood. The said Wood Inspectors shall each keep a receipt book in which they shall enter (in ink) the names of the owners of wood and the amount of the same, inspected by them; this entry shall be made upon the margin of the book, together with the date, and the hour when such inspection was made. The owner of the wood must in every instance surrender to the purchaser of the wood, the certificate received by him from the Wood Inspector.

SEC. 12. Any Inspector who shall be guilty of taking or demanding more compensation for his services than is prescribed by this Ordinance, or who shall be guilty of any fraud or peculation, in his office, shall, in addition to the punishment hereinafter prescribed, be removed from office by the Mayor or Common Council.

SEC. 13. Any violation of, or failure to comply with the provisions of this Ordinance, shall be punished by a fine not to exceed one hundred dollars and costs; and in the imposition of any such fine and costs, the Court may make a further sentence, that the offender be committed to the County Jail or Detroit House of Correction until the payment thereof, for any period of time not exceeding six months.

SEC. 14. Every wagon, cart or sleigh load of firewood brought to the City of Detroit for sale at the public wood-yards, and all firewood brought to the City by vessel, before the same shall be offered for sale, shall be subject to the inspection of Inspectors of Firewood of the Eastern or Western, or Northern or Southern District, as the case may be; and in case of a refusal of the person or persons in charge of said wood to have said wood inspected, and to pay the Inspector his lawful fees when demanded for such inspection, he or they shall be liable to the pains and penalties in section 13 of this chapter.

SEC. 15. Nothing in this chapter contained shall be made applicable to the Detroit City Water Works, but in all cases where wood is purchased for the use of said Water Works, it shall be optional with the seller and buyer to have the same inspected or not.

CHAPTER 24.

CHIMNEY SWEEPERS.

[Chapter Nineteen of the Revised Ordinances of 1863]

SECTION 1. There shall be nominated by the Mayor of the City of Detroit, subject to the approval of the Common Council, one Chimney Sweeper for the City, who shall have full power to appoint others under him, according to the subsequent provisions of this chapter.

SEC. 2. No person shall hereafter follow the business or occupation of a Chimney Sweeper, either by himself, or others, within the City of Detroit, unless he shall have been approved in the manner prescribed in section one, and shall give bonds to the City of Detroit, conditioned for the faithful performance of his duties, according to the provisions hereinafter contained, and shall have registered his name, and the names of all persons employed by him as assistants, with a number affixed to every such name, in a book to be kept by the City Clerk, and shall have obtained from said Clerk a certificate of such registry, containing the name of the person and the number affixed in said registry, under a penalty of five dollars for every day he shall follow, by himself or others, the said business; and the said Clerk is hereby required to make out and deliver to the person so appointed such certificates, for each of which he shall be entitled to demand and receive one dollar.

SEC. 3. Every person following the aforesaid business within said City, shall wear, and cause to be worn by the persons employed by him, on the front of their caps or hats, in full view, the same figures and numbers, respectively, as shall be so, as aforesaid, entered in the said book, and contained in his or their respective certificates, in large figures, not less than two inches in length, to be made of durable tin or copper, with the word "Sweep" legibly painted on said badge. Every person who shall violate the provisions of this section, shall forfeit one dollar.

SEC. 4. Every such Chimney Sweep, so appointed, who shall not, within forty-eight hours after application to him, made by any inhabitant of the district to which he belongs, sweep, or cause to be swept, such chimney, or chimneys, as he shall be required to sweep, shall, for every such offense, forfeit and pay the sum of three dollars.

SEC. 5. Each Chimney Sweeper so appointed, shall be entitled to demand and receive, for each chimney so swept, the following sums, and no more, to wit: For each chimney with a single flue the sum of twenty-five cents for every story through which such flue shall pass, and for each additional flue ten cents. [*As amended by Ordinance approved April 2, 1870.*]

SEC. 6. If any chimney in this City shall take fire, and blaze out at the top (the same not having been swept within three months next before the time of taking fire), the occupant of such premises shall forfeit and pay the sum of one dollar and costs. But if the same shall have been swept within three months, then the person having swept the same shall forfeit and pay one dollar and costs.

SEC. 7. Any violation of, or neglect, or refusal to comply, with the provisions of section two of this Ordinance, shall be punished by a fine not to exceed one hundred dollars and costs of prosecution; and in the imposition of any fine and costs the Court may make a further sentence that the offender be imprisoned until the payment thereof: *Provided*, That the term of such imprisonment shall not exceed the period of three months. [*Added by Ordinance approved April 30, 1866.*]

CHAPTER 25.

SUPERINTENDENT OF PARKS.

[Ordinance approved November 30, 1869.]

SECTION 1. Whenever any labor is performed in any of the Public Parks of said City, under the supervision of the Superintendent of Parks, it shall be the duty of said Superintendent of

Parks to present to the City Controller the proper pay-roll therefor, with an affidavit of said Superintendent indorsed on the back thereof, stating that the persons named in said pay-roll actually performed the work as therein charged; that the time mentioned therein was actually and necessarily employed in the performance of said work; that said labor was performed exclusively for the benefit of the corporation of the City of Detroit, and that the amount stated in said pay-roll for said work is just, true and correct. And the said Superintendent shall preserve in his office a duplicate of each pay-roll presented, with the duplicate number and copy of the affidavit indorsed thereon.

SEC. 2. When the Controller shall have issued his warrant upon the City Treasurer, for the payment of the amount due in said pay-rolls, it shall be the duty of the said Superintendent, within six days thereafter, to give the person entitled thereto an order upon the City Treasurer, from a book to be provided for that purpose, and to be kept in his, the Superintendent's office, which said order shall contain the number of the pay-roll, the district, and name of the park in which the work was performed, the number of days actually employed, the rate *per diem*, the amount due, and the person to whom the compensation is to be paid, as per pay-roll. The said Superintendent shall retain in said book in his office, for public inspection, a duplicate copy or stub of each order issued. Upon the presentation of said order to the City Treasurer, that officer shall pay to the person named in said order and pay-roll, and to no other, the amount stated therein to be due.

SEC. 3. Any failure to comply with the provisions of this Ordinance shall be punished by a fine not exceeding fifty dollars and costs; and in the imposition of such fine and costs, the Court may make a further sentence, that the offender be imprisoned in the Detroit House of Correction until the payment of such fine and costs: *Provided*, however, that such imprisonment shall not exceed the period of three months.

CHAPTER 26.

STANDING COMMITTEES.

[Chapter Twenty-one of the Revised Ordinances of 1863.]

SECTION 1. The following shall be the duties of Standing Committees of the Common Council, to wit:

1. The Committee on Claims shall examine into and report upon all matters of account or claim, either in favor of or against the City.

2. The Committee on Ways and Means shall examine into and report upon all such matters relative to the revenue of the City, as shall be referred to them; they shall inquire into the state of the City debt, the revenue, and the expenditures of the City; and whether any or what retrenchment can be made with advantage; and shall report, from time to time, such provisions and arrangements as may be promotive of order, economy and accountability in the conduct of the fiscal concerns of the City. They shall examine into and report upon the sufficiency of all official bonds, and all such matters not constituting a claim against the City, as shall be referred to them, and shall, with the City Controller, make and report the estimates for the yearly expenditures.

3. The Committee on Streets shall examine into and report upon all such matters as may be referred to them, relative to streets, alleys and sidewalks within the City, and shall, at the end of each year, report to the Common Council what improvements of any nature will be needed upon the streets, alleys and sidewalks of the City, during the ensuing year, and an estimate of the expenses of the same.

4. The Committee on Health shall examine into and report upon all matters relating to, or in any way affecting the Public Health, which shall be referred to them; and it shall be their duty to report, from time to time, to the Common Council, such plans and suggestions relative to the cleanliness and health of the City as they may deem proper.

5. The Committee on Fire Limits shall examine into and report upon all matters connected with the Fire Limits of the City, which may be referred to them. [*Amended by Act of Legislature creating Board Fire Commissioners.*]

6. The Committee on Hydraulics shall examine into and report upon the condition of the Hydraulics of the City, whenever so directed by the Common Council; and to them shall be referred all reports and communications from the Board of Commissioners of the Water Works.

7. The Committee on Markets shall examine into and report upon all matters connected with the Public Markets which may be referred to them.

8. The Committee on Taxes shall examine into and report upon all questions brought before the Common Council concerning Taxes, which may be referred to them.

9. The Committee on Printing shall examine into and report upon all matters connected with the City Printing, which may be referred to them. They shall also, at the end of the year, report to the Common Council an estimate of the expense necessary for the City Printing in the ensuing year.

10. The Committee on Gas Lights shall report upon all matters connected with the lighting of the City, which may be referred to them. To them shall be referred all reports of the Gas Company; and they shall, at the end of each year, report to the Common Council, the number, location, and cost of lights which will be necessary in the ensuing year.

11. The Committee on Public Buildings shall examine into and report upon the condition of all buildings belonging to the City; all questions and plans for repairs, erection and construction of public buildings, shall be referred to them; and they shall, at the end of each year, report to the Common Council the estimated expenses of their department for the ensuing year.

12. The Committee on Parks shall examine into and report upon the condition of all Public Parks; upon the improvements, adornment and protection thereof; and shall, at the end of each year, report the estimated expenses of their department during the ensuing year.

13. The Committee on Sewers shall examine into and report upon all questions connected with the construction of Sewers, which may be referred to them.

14. The Committee on Licenses shall examine into and report upon all questions connected with Licenses, which may be referred to them.

15. The Committee on National Affairs shall examine into and report upon all matters relating to the Federal Government, which may be referred to them.

16. The Committee on Education shall examine into, and report upon the condition and wants of our Public Schools, whenever they may deem it advisable to do so, or when questions appertaining thereto are referred to them. [*Amended by Session Laws of 1869.*]

17. The Committee on Judiciary shall examine into and report upon all questions involving points of law, the official conduct of persons presiding over Municipal Courts, and City Officers generally, which may be referred to them.

18. The Committee on House of Correction shall examine into and report upon all matters which may be referred to them relative to the management of the House of Correction; and, from time to time, also report such improvements respecting the same as they may deem advisable.

19. The Committee on Police shall examine into and report upon all matters appertaining to the management of the Police Department of the City, the official conduct of any of its officers, and all other questions relating to Police matters which may be referred to them." [*As amended by Ordinance approved March 7, 1868.*

SEC. 2. Every Committee, in the discharge of their duty, may require the services of any officer of the City, whose duties are in any manner connected with the subject under investigation by the Committee.

SEC. 3. No Committee shall exercise any executive functions, nor perform any duty save that usual to legislative bodies; nor shall they in any case order the doing of any work, or the cessation thereof, enter into any contract, or change or vary one already made; and any act performed by them, which is unauthorized by this Ordinance, shall be null and void.

SEC. 4. The Common Council shall always refer matters to the appropriate Committee; nor shall any matter be referred to a Committee which does not directly relate to the department which that Committee has been appointed to.

CHAPTER 27.

TAKING TESTIMONY BEFORE COMMITTEES.

[Chapter Twenty-two of the Revised Ordinances of 1863.]

SECTION 1. The presiding officer of any Board, or the Chairman of any Committee of the Common Council, who are engaged in the consideration, or to whom have been referred the investigation of any claim for damages, money or recompense against said Board, or against the City, may issue subpœnas under their hands, and sealed with the corporate seal of said City, directed to any person whom said Board or Committee deem necessary as a witness in any matter pending before them, and ordering said person to appear before said Committee or Board at such time and place, and to testify concerning such matter or thing, as in said subpœna shall be designated.

SEC. 2. If the person so subpœnaed shall fail to appear at said time and place, an attachment shall be issued to compel his appearance, which attachment shall be signed and sealed, as is provided for subpœnas in the preceding section.

SEC. 3. The person or party making such claim shall be entitled to a hearing before said Board or Committee, and to process to compel the appearance of witnesses in his behalf.

SEC. 4. The Members of the Metropolitan Police shall serve all process issuing under this Ordinance. Said process shall be served in the manner like processes are served in Courts of Justices of the Peace, and shall be returned to the presiding officer or chairman issuing them: *Provided always*, That in case of the absence of the Chairman of any Committee, the person whose name appears next to his in the order of appointment of said Committee, shall act as Chairman, and may issue all processes herein provided for.

SEC. 5 The statements of all persons concerning any such claim, made before any Board or Committee, as herein provided, shall, in all cases, be taken under oath, and reduced to writing by the Chairman of said Committee or presiding officer of said Board, and signed by the person making the same, which statement, so signed, shall be returned by the Chairman of said Committee to the City Attorney, who shall file and preserve the same in his office, subject to the order of the Common Council.

CHAPTER 28.

OFFICERS TO RECEIPT FOR MONEYS.

[Ordinance Approved March 3, 1865.]

SECTION 1. The City Treasurer, the Receiver of Taxes, City Collector, and Ward Collectors, are hereby required to execute and deliver a proper receipt to each and every person paying money to them for taxes or other purposes; also, to mark the tax, lien, claim or assessment, with the word "paid," writing the date of such payment immediately thereafter, in presence of the person to whom the receipt may be given, in the book, roll, or record thereof.

TITLE II.

TAXES AND ASSESSMENTS.

CHAPTER 29.

ASSESSMENT AND COLLECTION OF TAXES.

[Chapter Twenty of the Revised Ordinances of 1863.]

SECTION 1. It shall be the duty of the City Attorney to meet with the Assessors, and give them all necessary advice relative to the manner of making the general assessment, and if any property belonging to the Corporation should be assessed, to request that the same should be stricken from the roll.

SEC. 2. That whenever it shall be necessary to call a meeting of the freemen of said city, for the purpose of authorizing the said Common Council to assess or lay a tax on the real and personal property, within the limits of said City, the notice or proclamation for convening such meeting, shall be left or filed with the City Clerk, who shall cause a copy thereof to be duly published in said City, in one of the City papers, and in handbills.

SEC. 3. If such meeting shall authorize the Common Council to assess and levy any such tax, the chairman or other officer of the meeting shall certify the same to the Common Council, as soon as may be, and such authority so certified shall be recorded in the Journal, and filed by the City Clerk.

SEC. 4. Whenever any tax roll for city, highway, sewer and school taxes shall be placed in the hands of any Ward Collector, or the City Collector, by the Receiver of Taxes, in accordance with section twelve, of chapter nine, of the City Charter, said Collector shall proceed to collect the amounts appearing unpaid thereon, and shall make returns to the Receiver of Taxes, as commanded in the warrant annexed to said tax roll. The following shall be a sufficient form of warrant:

FORM OF WARRANT.

STATE OF MICHIGAN, } ss.
CITY OF DETROIT, }

To —— Collector of the —— Ward of the City of Detroit, Greeting:

In the name of the people of the State of Michigan, You are hereby commanded, that you collect from the several persons named in the foregoing Tax Roll, or of any person liable to pay the same, the amount of highway, sewer, school and city taxes opposite to their names respectively, together with —— per cent for your services for collecting the same; and on the neglect or refusal of any such person to pay such taxes, that you then levy the same by distress and sale of goods and chattels of such person, occupant, or lessee refusing or neglecting to pay the same, according to law; and that you have said roll, and the money so collected by you, and this warrant, before the Receiver of Taxes of said City, on the —— day of —— 18—.

In testimony whereof, I have hereunto set my hand and caused the seal of said City to be affixed, at the City of Detroit [L S] aforesaid, this —— day of —— A. D. 18—.

———— *Controller.*

Sec. 5. In case of levy and sale, in accordance with section thirteen, of chapter nine, of the City Charter, the following shall be a sufficient form of notice of sale of property levied upon. Any such sale may be adjourned from time to time by the Collector making the same.

NOTICE OF SALE OF PROPERTY.

STATE OF MICHIGAN, } ss.
CITY OF DETROIT, }

Notice is hereby given, that, pursuant to law in such case made and provided, there will be sold at public auction, to the highest bidder, at —— ——, in the City of Detroit, at —— o'clock, in the —— noon of —— day of —— A. D. 18—, the following goods and chattels, viz: [here description] or so much thereof as may be necessary to satisfy the amount of —— taxes imposed upon

—— —— for the year 18—, and which are to be levied by said sale.

Dated at Detroit, this —— day of —— A. D. 18—.

——— *Collector for—— City of Detroit.*

SEC. 6. The following shall be a sufficient form of return:

COLLECTOR'S RETURN.

STATE OF MICHIGAN, } ss.
CITY OF DETROIT, }

To the Receiver of Taxes of said City of Detroit:

The undersigned begs leave to submit the following list of persons named in the annexed assessment roll, who were taxed for the year 18—, upon personal property, according to the assessment roll of said City, and the taxes imposed upon such persons, which I have been unable to collect:

NAMES.	TAX.		
	DOLLS.	CENTS.	

Given at the City of Detroit, this —— day of —— A. D. 18—.

——— *Collector for —— City of Detroit.*

STATE OF MICHIGAN, } ss.
CITY OF DETROIT, }

——— ———, Collector of the —— Ward of said City, being duly sworn, deposes and says that the several sums mentioned in the foregoing returns of the city, school, highway and sewer taxes for the year 18—, remain due and unpaid, and that he has not, upon diligent inquiry, been able to discover any goods and chattels belonging to the persons charged with or liable to pay said sums of money whereon he could levy the same.

———*Collector for——City of Detroit.*

Subscribed and sworn before me this —— day of —— A. D. 18—.

——— *Clerk of said City.*

CHAPTER 30.

SALE OF LANDS FOR UNPAID TAXES AND ASSESSMENTS.

[Chapter Twenty-four of the Revised Ordinances of 1863.]

SECTION 1. Whenever any general tax or assessment on any lands, tenements, hereditaments or premises in said City, shall remain due and unpaid, after publication of notice by the Receiver of Taxes, as required by the provisions of section twelve, chapter nine, of the Charter, and after the expiration of the time therein mentioned, it shall be the duty of the Receiver of Taxes, on behalf of the Common Council, to proceed and sell such lands, tenements, hereditaments and premises, in the manner herein prescribed.

SEC. 2. The Receiver of Taxes shall, on or before the first day of May in each year, make out a list of all such lands, tenements, hereditaments or premises, the names, if known, of the owners or occupants of, or parties in interest, and the amount of the unpaid tax or assessment due thereon, and shall, on behalf of the Common Council, cause to be published in the daily newspaper published by the Printer for the City, once a week for four successive weeks, such list with a notice thereto attached, requiring the owners or occupants of, or parties in interest in such lands, tenements, hereditaments or premises, to pay any such assessment or tax; and further notifying them that if default be made in making any such payment, any such real estate will be sold, at public auction, at a day and place therein to be specified, for the lowest term of years at which any person will offer to take the same, in consideration of advancing and paying the sum assessed or taxed on the same, with the costs and charges in the premises, and shall, at the same time, cause said list, with said notice thereto attached, to be posted in three or more public places in each Ward in said City. [*As amended by Ordinance approved December 12, 1870.*]

SEC. 3. If the owner or owners, occupant or occupants, party or parties in interest, in any such real estate, do not pay any such assessment or tax, with the costs and charges thereon, within the period above prescribed for the publication of said notice, then the Receiver of Taxes, on behalf of the Common Council, at the place, and on the day mentioned in such notice, shall commence the sale of such lands, tenements, hereditaments and premises, at public auction, and shall continue the same from day to day (Sundays excepted), until the same is sold for the lowest term of years at which any person shall offer to take the same, for the purpose, and in the manner already above expressed; but each lot, or parcel of lot, owned by any one person, or set of persons, against whom any such tax or assessment has been made, shall be sold by itself.

SEC. 4. The Receiver of Taxes shall report to the Common Council, within ten days after the close of such sale, the terms for which each lot was sold, the amount bid therefor, and the name of the purchaser; and if there be no sufficient objection, the several purchasers shall, on payment of the amount of their respective bids, as hereinafter provided, be entitled to the necessary conveyances of said premises, when the time for the redemption, fixed by law, shall have fully expired, upon paying for the expense of such conveyance the further sum of fifty cents, unless said lot shall have been sooner redeemed, in which case the purchaser shall be entitled to recover his money and interest, at the rates hereinafter established.

SEC. 5. The purchasers at such sale shall pay the amount of their respective bids to the Receiver of Taxes, within forty-eight hours after the sale has been finally closed, and, on payment of the same, it shall be the duty of the Receiver of Taxes, on behalf of the Common Council, to execute to the purchaser of each lot a proper certificate of such sale, describing the lands purchased, and the amount paid therefor, and the term of years for which the same was bid off; and such certificate shall be regularly numbered, and a copy of each shall be filed in the office of the Controller.

SEC. 6. The Receiver of Taxes may, in his discretion, require immediate payment of any person to whom any such real estate shall be struck off, and in case of his neglect or refusal to pay any bid made by him, he may declare the bid canceled, and, at his discretion, sell the lands again, and any person so neglecting or refusing to pay any bid made by him, shall not be entitled, after such neglect and refusal, to have any bid made by him received during such sale.

SEC. 7. If any purchaser shall neglect or refuse to pay the amount of their respective bids to the Receiver of Taxes, within forty-eight hours after the sale, the Receiver of Taxes shall report the names of such persons to the Common Council, who may elect to take the lots bid off by such purchaser.

SEC. 8. On presentation of certificate of sale, heretofore referred to, the Controller, after the expiration of the time provided by law for the redemption of real estate, sold as aforesaid, unless such real estate has been previously redeemed, the Controller shall, in the name of, and for the City of Detroit, execute and deliver to such purchaser, or his assignee, a proper deed for the conveyance of such real estate, for the term for which the same was sold, which said deed shall be under the corporate seal of the City, and attested by the Clerk.

SEC. 9. The Receiver of Taxes, within forty days after such sale, shall make a correct record of all land sales, showing the time when the tax or assessment was levied, and the amount thereof, the cost and charges, the time when the lands were sold, the name of the purchaser, or his assignee, the term for which the same was bid off, with such other entries as may be necessary in the premises, and shall deposit said record in the office of the Treasurer.

SEC. 10. Any person entitled to redeem any such real estate, may, within one year from the time of sale, deposit with the Treasurer, for the use of the purchaser, the full amount of the assessment, or tax, for which such real estate was sold, and interest, as hereinafter mentioned, and the Treasurer shall give proper receipt for the same, and shall enter a note of such redemption in said record. Interest on unpaid taxes shall be at the rate of twelve per cent per annum, up to, and until the date of the sale of such real estate, and at the rate of twenty-five per cent per annum from and after such sale, and no person shall be entitled, after sale, to redeem any real estate sold without payment of the said interest and principal, in the manner prescribed by law.

SEC. 11. If, on the day mentioned in such notice of sale, the Receiver of Taxes shall neglect, or be unable, from any cause, to be present at, and conduct said sale, then it shall be the duty of the Treasurer, in behalf of the Common Council, to proceed with said sale, in the same manner, and with the like effect, as if the same had been conducted by the Receiver of Taxes, and he shall receive payments of bids, make the like returns, issue certificates of purchase, and make out the same record, and perform all other acts, as are required of the Receiver of Taxes, under like circumstances.

SEC. 12. The following, or other sufficient forms, may be used in proceedings under this chapter:

NOTICE OF SALE.

STATE OF MICHIGAN, } ss.
CITY OF DETROIT. }

Notice is hereby given, that pursuant to law, there will be sold at the Common Council Hall, in the City of Detroit, and State of Michigan, between the hours of —— and ——, of the ——— day of———, A. D. 18—, at public auction, the several lands, tenements, hereditaments, and premises, hereinafter described, each parcel separately, for the lowest term of years at which any person will offer to take the same, in consideration of advancing the sum or sums which were assessed or taxed by the Common Council of said City, for the year 18—, unless the said sum, or sums, with the costs and charges thereon, shall, before that time, be paid and satisfied, which the owners, or occupants of, or parties in interest in said lands, tenements, hereditaments and premises, against whom said sum or sums have been assessed, are hereby required to do. [Here insert an accurate description of the several premises, and add to the description of each the amount assessed, the name of the individual or individuals against whom the amount is assessed, and also the amount of the costs and charges, if any, up to that time.]

NAMES.	DESCRIPTION OF LOTS.	AMOUNT OF TAX.	COSTS AND CHARGES.

Dated at the City of Detroit, this —— day of —— A. D. 18—.
By order of the Common Council.

—— ——, *Receiver of Taxes.*

CHAPTER 31.

OF THE COLLECTION OF TAXES AND SALE OF LANDS FOR UNPAID SPECIAL ASSESSMENTS.

[Ordinance approved December 5, 1870.]

SECTION 1. Whenever any assessment roll for any special assessment has been approved and sonfirmed by the Common Council the same shall be deposited with the Receiver of Taxes, who shall retain the same in his office for the period of thirty days, or such further period of time as the Common Council shall by resolution direct, during which period the persons assessed may pay to him the respective amounts of their assessments.

SEC. 2. At the expiration of the said period of time, as prescribed in section one, the rolls shall be placed in the hands of the Collector, with a warrant similar in form to the one prescribed in chapter twenty-nine of these Ordinances, but returnable in sixty days from the date thereof, directing him to collect all sums unpaid thereon, and also five per cent in addition to defray the expenses of collection, and one per cent per month in addition thereto on the amount of each assessment from the time he received the rolls to the time when the same is paid or collected.

SEC. 3. Upon all sums collected and paid to the contractor or other officer, who performs any work or service for which any special assessment shall be made, there shall (in all cases where the said one per cent per month has been paid into the City Treasury) also be paid to such contractor, or officer, on all sums paid for principal, interest thereon at the rate of seven per cent per annum for the period for which such one per cent per month has been paid or collected, which shall be in full for all claims for interest on such assessments, under any contract with the City.

SEC. 4. Upon the reception of the warrant above provided for, the Collector shall proceed to execute and return the same, in like manner as provided for the collection of City taxes. Upon the return thereof unsatisfied, in whole or in part, the Receiver of Taxes shall proceed to advertise and sell, and take such subsequent proceedings as provided in case of unpaid City taxes.

SEC. 5. Said warrant may be renewed from time to time by direction of the Common Council.

SEC. 6. It shall be the duty of the Receiver of Taxes to receive payment of taxes on a part of any lot, tract or parcel of land, or on any undivided share or other interest therein, which the tax payer will clearly define. Upon such payment the said Receiver shall mark the same paid upon the proper roll, and give the party making the same a receipt therefor. Said Receiver shall also specify on said roll, the part, share or interest of said lot, tract or parcel on which said tax is paid.

SEC. 7. If the part on which the tax is so paid, shall be an undivided share, the person paying the same shall state to the Receiver the name of the owner of share, that it may be exempted from sale, in case of a sale for tax on the remainder, for which purpose the Receiver shall enter the name and interest of such owner on the proper roll.

SEC. 8. Any portion of a lot, tract or a parcel of land, or any undivided share, or other interest therein, which may be clearly defined, and which has been sold for the payment of any tax or assessment, may be redeemed at any time within one year succeeding the sale, by the owner thereof depositing with the City Treasurer his just proportion of the amount for which the whole lot, tract or parcel was sold, together with the interest and charges thereon.

SEC. 9. All insurance companies who do business and have

agencies in the City of Detroit shall pay as a tax the sum of one per cent upon the amount of premiums upon all policies issued: *Provided, however,* That no such tax shall be levied upon premiums for insurance upon property owned and situated without the limits of said City at the date when such policy issued, or such premium was paid or contracted to be paid.

SEC. 10. It shall be the duty of every agent or agents, or other principal officer or officers having charge or control of the business of any such insurance company located or doing business in said City, to, within ten days after service of the notice hereinafter provided for, make a true return under oath to the City Assessor, showing the gross amount received by the company or companies for which he or they are agents, or controlling officers, for premiums such as are specified in section number nine of this Ordinance for the six months ending the first day of September, A. D. 1870, and the first days of March and September in each year thereafter, provided that returns need not be made for policies issued upon property located outside of the City limits.

SEC. 11. It is hereby made the duty of the City Assessor to give to all persons doing the business of insurance within the limits of said city, as agents or controlling officers, a written or printed notice to make and file with such Assessor a full and complete statement, under oath, showing the gross amount received by the company or companies for which he or they are agents or officers, for premiums such as specified in section nine of this Ordinance, for the period of six months next preceding the first day of September and the first day of March in each year, previous to the service of such notice. Such notices shall be served as follows, viz: For the six months preceding the first of September, 1870, within ten days after the passage of this Ordinance, and thereafter on the first day of March and September in each year, or as soon thereafter as may be.

SEC. 12 It shall be the duty of said Assessor to assess the said insurance companies respectively upon the returns of their officers and agents, as provided for in this Ordinance, and to report to the Common Council a full statement thereof, on or before the first Tuesday in November and May in each and every year, and in case returns are not made according to the provisions of this Ordinance by all insurance companies the Assessor shall assess the companies neglecting or refusing to make such returns at the rate of one per cent upon the amount of premiums they shall have received according to his best judgment and information. And in case the amount so assessed shall be unsatisfactory to the company thus assessed, they may appear before the Board of Review or Common Council, who shall correct the same as shall be deemed just.

SEC. 13. The assessment roll for the insurance taxes hereby provided for, when accepted and confirmed by the Common Council, shall be placed in the hands of the Receiver of Taxes for collection, and shall be collected in the same manner as taxes for personal property are now levied and collected.

SEC. 14. All taxes collected under the provisions of this Ordinance shall be credited to the Fire Department Fund, and paid into the same.

SEC. 15. In case any agent, or other principal officer having charge or control of the business of any insurance company, as mentioned in this Ordinance, shall fail to make return of the amount of premiums upon policies issued upon property as aforesaid, or deliver to the City Assessor a statement under oath, as prescribed in section ten of this Ordinance, such offender shall be punished by a fine not to exceed three hundred dollars and costs; and in the imposition of any such fine and costs the court may make a further sentence, that the offender be imprisoned in the Detroit House of Correction until the payment thereof, for any period of time not exceeding six (6) months.

CHAPTER 32.

DISPOSITION OF BIDS BY THE CITY FOR LANDS SOLD FOR TAXES OR ASSESSMENTS.

[Chapter twenty-seven of the Revised Ordinances of 1863.]

SECTION 1. Whenever any lands, bid in for the City under the provisions of section twenty-one of chapter nine of the Revised Charter of said City of the year 1857, shall not be redeemed by the owner or other persons interested in said lands, within one year from the day on which said lands are so bid in, it shall be lawful for the City Treasurer, and he is hereby authorized to sell, assign and transfer to any person or persons who shall pay the tax or assessment, together with the costs and charges for which said land was sold, all the interest which the City has acquired in said land by reason of said bid. And he shall give to the person or persons who shall so pay said tax or assessment, together with said costs and charges, a certificate of the fact of such payment, in which certificate the land or lands for which such payment is made shall be particularly described.

SEC. 2. Upon presentation to him of the certificate provided for in the foregoing section, the City Controller shall, under the seal of the City, execute to the person named in the certificate a full and absolute assignment and transfer of the conveyance or certificate of sale of the land or lands for which the person or persons named in said certificate of the Treasurer shall have made said payment.

SEC. 3. It shall be the duty of the City Treasurer, whenever persons bidding for lands at any sale for delinquent taxes or assessments, shall fail to pay the amount of their said bid, to report the fact to the Common Council.

CHAPTER 33.

THE SALE OF LOTS HELD BY THE CITY UNDER TAX TITLES, AND CANCELING DEFECTIVE TAX TITLES.

[Chapter One Hundred of the Revised Ordinances of 1863.]

SECTION 1. The Treasurer is authorized to advertise and sell and convey all the right, title and interest of the City in and to the several lots and premises held through tax titles by the City, giving three months' notice of the time and place of sale, in two or more newspapers published in the City, and by publishing a list or description of said lands in handbill form, for general distribution through the several Wards; the expense thereof to be added to the sum fixed as a minimum price for said lots. The Sergeant of Police shall cause said handbills to be posted in ten public places in each Ward thirty days before said sale. Any lot or parcel of land not sold and paid for at said sale may, at any time thereafter, be sold and disposed of at private sale at the minimum price. [*As amended by Ordinance approved December 12, 1870.*]

SEC. 2. The City Treasurer shall, in all cases wherein satisfactory evidence shall be presented to him of erroneous assessment or return or sale, of any lot or premises, be authorized to receive the original tax, with interest at seven per cent from the day of sale, in compromise of the claims of the City for its tax title to any such lot or premises: *Provided,* The same shall be approved by the Controller.

SEC. 3. It shall be the duty of the City Treasurer, whenever satisfactory evidence is presented to him of the payment of any tax on any lot or parcel of land, to discharge said premises from said tax, if the same has not been sold; and if the same has been sold to the City, he shall cancel or quit-claim to the owner the tax title thus acquired; and if the tax thus paid has not been accounted for and paid over by the officer receiving said tax, the Treasurer shall immediately cause proceedings to be taken for the collection of the same.

SEC. 4. If any tax upon any lot or parcel of land shall be twice paid, the City Treasurer may, with the approval of the Common Council and the Controller, refund one of said payments to the party entitled thereto.

CHAPTER 34.

ILLEGAL TAXES AND ASSESSMENTS.

[Ordinance approved December 5, 1863.]

SECTION 1. Whenever it shall appear to the satisfaction of the Common Council of the City of Detroit, that any City Tax has been illegally assessed or collected, the said Council may, by a vote of two-thirds of all members elected, direct and cause such tax or assessment, if collected, to be repaid, in whole or in part, to the person or persons from whom collected, out of the Contingent Fund; and if such tax or assessment has not been collected, said Council may, by a like vote of two-thirds, direct and cause the same to be vacated or stricken from the rolls; when so vacating any tax or assessment, the Council may require as a condition precedent, the payment into the city treasury of a sum to be fixed by the Council; any sum so paid shall be credited to the same fund into which such tax or assessment would have been paid if collected in full.

SEC. 2. No action had under this Ordinance shall in any way affect or invalidate any other tax or assessment assessed, levied or collected in said City.

TITLE III.

STREETS, ALLEYS AND PUBLIC PLACES.

CHAPTER 35.

PAVING STREETS AND ALLEYS.

[Ordinance approved November 29, 1869.]

SECTION 1. Streets, or parts thereof, may be ordered to be graded and paved, by resolution of the Common Council, on motion of any member thereof, at a total cost to be expended in any one year, not exceeding one hundred and fifty thousand dollars. Such resolution shall in each case specify the intent to act under this power.

SEC. 2. Streets, or parts thereof, may also be ordered to be graded and paved, by resolution of the Common Council, on petition of parties owning a majority of property fronting on the line of such street, or the part thereof proposed to be paved. Such primary petition shall pray generally that the street, or a specified part thereof, be graded and paved; and the preferences of the petitioners, or other parties interested, as to the kind of pavement they desire, may be shown by subsequent petition.

SEC. 3. When a street, or part thereof, is ordered to be graded and paved, the resolution shall declare generally that it is ordered that the street, within specified limits, be graded and paved; and shall direct what kind of pavement may be advertised for; and that for the purpose of assessment to defray the expense of such improvement, the lots and parcels of real estate situated upon such street, and fronting on the portion thereof ordered to be improved, shall constitute a local assessment district; or two or more assessment districts may be thus established, of not less extent than one block each, in the discretion of the Council.

SEC. 4. The City Surveyor, upon the passage of the resolution establishing a local assessment district, as provided in section three, shall forthwith proceed to ascertain the quantities of work and material requisite to the improvement so ordered, and to estimate and apportion the expense of advertising and blanks, and of inspection of the work during its progress; and shall make report of the same in duplicate, over his signature, as near as conveniently may be, according to form "A," hereto attached, and deliver one to the Controller and one to the Assessor.

FORM A.

(For the City Surveyor to report Quantities to the Controller and Assessor:)

CITY SURVEYOR'S OFFICE,
DETROIT, —— 18—.

Quantities for grading, paving, etc., ——, from the —— line of —— to the —— line of ——, exclusive of the quantities within the lines of the cross streets and alleys.

	QUANTITIES.	DESCRIPTION OF WORK.	
	Cubic yards............	Excavation...............	
	Lineal feet	Curb stone...............	
	Square yards	Paving	

	DOLL'S.	CENTS.
Proportion of cost of advertising and blanks, to be paid by tax		
Proportion of Inspector's compensation, to be paid by tax...		

FOR THE CITY.

The quantities within the lines of the intersections of the cross streets and alleys, and the crosswalks within such intersections:

	QUANTITIES.	DESCRIPTION OF WORK.	
	Cubic yards............	Excavation..............	
	Lineal feet	Curb stone...............	
	Square yards............	Paving	
	Square feet	Stone culvert platform	
	Square feet	Wooden " "	
	Square feet	Rec'g basin "	
	....	....	
	....	....	
	Square feet	Crosswalks...............	

	DOLL'S.	CENTS.
City's proportion of cost of advertising and blanks.........		
City's proportion of Inspector's compensation		

I certify that the above quantities and estimates are correct.

City Surveyor.

SEC. 5. It shall be the duty of the Controller, as soon as he receives the report of the Surveyor, in Section 4, above provided for, to proceed to advertise fifteen days, unless otherwise ordered by resolution of the Common Council, in the official city paper, for bids for the making such improvement, with the kinds of pavement he shall have been directed to advertise for by the Council, and as required by section 207 of the City Charter of 1857, and by Section 39 of Chapter 8 of said Charter as amended by Act of Legislature No. 486, approved April 5, 1869. Such advertisement shall specify a time and place when and where such bids shall be opened; at which time and place such bids shall be opened by the Controller, or his deputy, in the presence of such persons as shall choose to attend; and the Controller shall then report to the Council all the bids received for each kind of pavement advertised for, designating the lowest responsible bidder. [*As amended by Ordinance approved October 3, 1870.*]

SEC. 6. Upon presentation of the report of the Controller in Section 5, above provided, the Common Council may, by resolution, direct the Controller to contract with such of the lowest responsible bidders reported by the Controller, as it shall see fit; or direct further advertisement for the same, or different kinds of pavement, in its discretion; and then direct the Controller to contract with such lowest bidder, for such kind of pavement as is deemed expedient to adopt for the improvement.

SEC. 7. Upon the passage of the resolution in Section 6 above provided, the Controller shall forthwith proceed to enter into a contract with the party designated therein, and take sufficient security for its faithful performance. Such contract shall, among other things, provide: First, that the City shall pay for grading and paving the interior spaces at the intersection of cross-streets and alleys, and for the cross-walks within the limits of the contemplated improvement, when the same shall have been completed according to contract, at either crossing. Second, that the contractors shall be paid for the remainder of the improvement out of the moneys assessed and collected from the local assessment district, and that the City shall not be liable or responsible for the payment thereof. Third, that the contractors shall follow the direction of the Inspector of Pavement, as to the manner of doing the work, and abide his decision as to the quality of the material to be used in the same, where questions arise within the specifications of the contract as to compliance therewith ; subject only to appeal to the decision of the Controller, and Chairman of the Committee on Streets, in behalf of the contractors, whose decision upon such appeal shall be final, and the work be stopped at the point of question, till the requirements of such decision are complied with. Fourth, such contract shall contain such other provisions, usual in such contracts, as the Controller shall deem necessary and proper, and for the interest of the City, and as are required by the Ordinances and Charter; and when such contract is duly executed, the same shall be reported by the Controller to the Council for confirmation, and the Council may either confirm or reject the same, and require such additional provisions inserted as shall to it seem necessary, and after the same is amended and executed, shall confirm the same.

Sec. 8. It shall be the duty of the City Assessor, immediately on receiving the report of the Surveyor, in Section 4 of this Ordinance provided for, forthwith to proceed and make a list of property in the local assessment district which shall have been established by the Common Council according to section 3 of this Ordinance, as he is required to do by section 42 of the act amending the Charter, approved April 5, 1869, and shall have such list in readiness to make the assessment required by said section 42, by the time the contract mentioned in section 7 of this Ordinance shall have been confirmed by the Council, and immediately upon such confirmation last mentioned, he shall compute the total cost of the improvement, including expenses reported by the Surveyor, and proceed to make assessment of the same, and advertise, and correct the assessment, and report to the Common Council, as in said section 42 of said amendments to the Charter he is required, and the Common Council shall proceed, as in said section 42 it is provided, to the confirmation of such assessment; and upon confirmation of such assessment roll, the City Clerk shall deliver the same to the Controller.

Sec. 9. The Controller, upon receipt of said assessment roll in the last section provided, shall make the necessary entries in his books, as required by the Charter and Ordinances, and may retain the same in his office, in his discretion, until work under the contract which he shall have made is commenced; he shall at that time or at such time previous to the commencement of the work, as he shall deem expedient, deliver such assessment roll to the Receiver of Taxes; and thereafter, such proceedings shall be taken thereupon, as are provided in the Charter and Ordinances for the collection of special assessments.

SEC. 10. The Common Council may appoint an Inspector of Pavement to superintend the improvement in each local assessment district formed under this Ordinance, whose duty it shall be to superintend the work on such improvement, and see to it that all the specifications of the contract for the work are complied with, under the direction of the said employers. Such Inspector may be discharged in the discretion of said Common Council, and his compensation shall not exceed the rate of $3 per diem of ten hours' work, and to be paid out of the City Treasury, and out of the assessment on the local assessment district upon which he is employed, in the proportion that the time of his employment bears to the total estimate of the Surveyor for that purpose. And said Inspector, at the request of said Common Council, shall report the progress of the performance of the contract in sections, as required from time to time, to the end that payment may be made by installments as the work progresses. [*As amended by Ordinance approved November 5, 1870.*]

SEC. 11. The Controller shall, upon receiving the certificate of the Inspector of the completion of any portion of the improvement according to the terms of the contract, make report to the Common Council at its next regular meeting of the fact of such completion, and the proportion that such part bears to the whole contract price, together with a statement of the amount of money collected on such special assessment at the time of making such report; and the Council may, upon such report, direct the Controller to draw his warrant or warrants upon the proper funds, to pay the contractors the *pro rata* amount of money payable therefor, or such per centage of said *pro rata* amount as the Council shall deem meet; and when the contract is fully performed, the Controller and Chairman of the Committee on Streets shall report accordingly to the Council, and it may accept such performance, and order payment accordingly; but in no case shall such performance be accepted, or paid for, without such report.

SEC. 12. The cost of the improvement hereinbefore provided for, within the lines of the cross streets and alleys, and the cost of the crosswalks, shall be paid out of the General Road Fund of the City; and the remainder of such costs shall be paid from the assessments hereinbefore provided for.

SEC. 13. The same proceedings shall be adopted for the grading and paving of alleys as are herein provided with respect to streets; except that no alley shall be ordered paved, without petition of a majority of property holders thereon; nor shall a local assessment district, for grading and paving any alley, be constituted of more than one block.

SEC. 14. The various City officers whose duties are prescribed by this Ordinance, shall take official notice of the resolutions of the Common Council, which shall be passed under this Ordinance, and of the proceedings and reports of each other, herein provided for, and shall proceed to the discharge of their several duties in the order herein prescribed without further notice.

[Ordinance Approved June 10, 1869.]

SEC. 15. Whenever the Common Council shall determine that a street shall be paved in the City of Detroit, it shall be the duty of the Street Commissioners of the District in which such paving is to be done to serve or cause to be served a written, or partly written and partly printed, notice upon each and every one of the owners, occupants or agents of property along the line of such street where such pavement is proposed to be laid, requiring him, her or them, within ten days from the date of such notice, to make connections with the main water and gas pipes that may be laid in said street, except where such connections have already been made.

SEC. 16. If along the line of such street there is any vacant or unoccupied lot, lots or premises, and the owner, owners, agent or agents thereof cannot be conveniently found, the said Street Commissioners shall post such notice, as aforesaid, in some conspicuous place upon said lot, lots or premises.

SEC. 17. In case of default or neglect on the part of any owner, occupant or agent to connect with the service pipe, as aforesaid, or in case the notice posted on any vacant and unoccupied lot, lots or premises, shall fail to come to the notice of the owner, owners, agent or agents thereof, and such notice has expired, the City shall then cause such connections to be made, and the expense therefor shall be assessed upon the property for the benfit of which such connection was made, and such assessment shall be a lien upon the said property until paid, and such lien shall have the same force and effect as is provided for in case of other special assessments.

CHAPTER 36.

SIDEWALKS.

[Ordinance Approved November 29, 1869.]

SECTION 1. The Common Council may order, by resolution, the construction of any sidewalk required to be built in the City of Detroit; said walks shall be built under the supervision of the Street Commissioner of the proper district, and as follows: All walks laid down on Grand River street, from Woodward avenue to Cass avenue; on Michigan avenue, from Randolph street to Fifth street; on Shelby street, from Woodbridge street to Michigan avenue; on Third street, from Woodbridge street to Fort street; on Bates street, from the Detroit River to Michigan avenue; on Randolph street, from the Detroit River to Gratiot street; on Brush street, from Atwater street to Congress street; on Larned street, from Third street to Brush street; on Congress street, from Third street to St. Antoine street; on Washington avenue, from Michigan avenue to Grand Circus; on Woodbridge street, from Third street to Brush street; and on both sides of each and every one of the said streets, as far as designated above, shall be constructed of stone flagging, or patent concrete pavement, and of no other material; and all sidewalks hereafter laid down on Jefferson avenue, from Third street to Dequindre street; on Fort street, from Woodward avenue to Eighth street; on Woodward avenue, from the river to the south side of Park and Williams street; all sidewalks around the Campus Martius; on Monroe avenue, from Campus Martius to Randolph street; on Larned street, from Woodward avenue to Third street; on Congress street, from Woodward avenue to Third street; on Griswold street, from the river to Michigan avenue; and Lafayette street, from Michigan avenue to Fifth street, shall be constructed of stone flagging, and of no other material. All other walks shall be constructed of plank, or of material above specified: *Provided*, No sidewalk within the limits above mentioned shall be repaired with plank, except by permission of the Common Council.

SEC. 2. Stone walks shall be constructed as follows:

I. The stone flagging shall be laid upon six inches of clean sand, and in water lime.

II. Said flagging shall not be less than three inches in thickness, and not less than two feet square, and dressed even on the sides, so as to form close and even joints.

III. Old flagging, when good, may be re-cut and laid next to the curb or the building, but the central portion of the sidewalk, for not less than six feet in width, shall be laid with new flagging.

IV. The curbstones laid for the purpose of supporting the sidewalks shall not be less than thirty inches in length, four inches thick, and eighteen inches wide throughout; the top of the stone to be beveled so as to correspond with the inclination of the sidewalk; the front to be cut smooth; the ends, from top to bottom, to be truly squared, so as to form close and even joints.

V. The curbstones shall be set perpendicular, and in conformity to the established grade. At the intersection of streets with other streets, or with alleys, the curbstones shall be set upon a proper curve, and to the satisfaction of the City Surveyor and the Street Commissioner of the proper district.

VI. Concrete or coal tar sidewalks constructed under this Ordinance, shall be laid with a foundation not less than six inches in depth, of coarse gravel and crushed cinders, which shall be covered with a coat of cement not less than three inches in thickness.

Sec. 3. Plank sidewalks shall be constructed of good pine or oak plank, which shall not be less than two inches in thickness, nor more than twelve inches wide, on oak, cedar or hemlock sleepers, not less than four inches square, to be placed not more than three feet apart; the plank shall be laid in a line at right angles to the line of the sidewalk, and shall be nailed with nails not less than thirty-penny, with at least three in each end of each plank, and not less than two at any other bearing.

Sec. 4. All sidewalks shall be raised from the curbstone in the proportion of eight inches on twenty feet, and in conformity to the established grade.

Sec. 5. Walks on Jefferson, Woodward avenues, on Michigan avenue to Seventh street, and on Wayne street, from Fort street to Michigan avenue, shall not be less than twelve feet wide; on Washington avenue, not less than ten feet wide; on Grand River street, from Woodward avenue to Third street, not less than eight feet wide; on all other streets they shall not be less than six feet. [*See Chapters 44, 45.*]

Sec. 6. Whenever the Council shall order any sidewalk to be built, it shall be the duty of the Street Commissioner to notify the owner, agent or occupant of any lot in front of, or adjacent to which such walk is to be constructed, to build the same within ten days from the date of the notice. If such owner, agent or occupant shall neglect to build said walk, within the time specified in said notice, it shall be the duty of the Street Commissioner to at once cause the same to be done, in the manner herein provided, and the expense thereof shall be a lien upon the lot or premises in front of, or adjacent to which such walk is required to be built. The Street Commissioner shall enter in a book to be provided for that purpose, memoranda, with dates, names, etc., of all such notices served by him, and shall file and keep in his office copies of all such notices, with a return of the date and mode of service indorsed thereon.

SEC. 7. If from such return it appears that said sidewalks have not been built by the parties notified within the ten days prescribed, the said Street Commissioner shall thereupon notify the City Surveyor of such fact, whereupon the said Surveyor shall, with all due diligence, make out a written report or assessment roll, stating therein the names of the owners or occupants of the lots or premises in front of, or adjacent to which said sidewalks may be constructed, or directed so to be; describing by itself, with sufficient accuracy, each lot or portion of a lot owned by any one person or company of persons, and also the names of such owner or several owners (and when he cannot ascertain the names of any such owners or occupants, or either of them, he shall state such fact in his report), and the sum of money of which such person or set of persons shall be assessed at, and pay for such sidewalks, and also thirty cents for each description, to defray the expenses of making such assessment, which report the said City Surveyor shall present to said Common Council.

SEC. 8. The City Clerk shall then make out a notice, directed to the several persons in said report named and proposed to be assessed, notifying them that they are about to be assessed, to defray the expenses of constructing the sidewalks adjacent to certain premises owned or occupied by them in said City, and that a report or assessment roll made out in the premises is on file in the office of said Clerk, for inspection, and further notifying them of the time and place when the Common Council will meet and review said report or assessment, which said notice shall be published in some daily newspaper printed in said City, for four successive days. The said Common Council shall, at the time and place in said notice specified, or some session thereafter, take said assessment into consideration, and if no person appears to object to said report or roll, and no good cause to the contrary appears, and an affidavit of publication of the requisite notice having been made, they shall, by a written resolution, to be entered on their iournal, declare that they approve of said report or assessment roll, that they receive as correct the description of the premises, and the names of the individuals therein contained, and that the sum which said report states to be the correct one, which each individual or set of individuals should be assessed at and pay, be the assessment, and be collected from the respective persons liable, according to law ; and may cause such assessment roll to be so corrected as may be just and right in the premises.

SEC. 9. Upon the confirmation of such assessment roll, it shall be delivered to the Controller, and by him, when the work is completed, forthwith deposited with the Receiver of Taxes, who shall retain the same in his office for the period of thirty days, during which period the persons assessed may pay to him the respective amounts of their assessments. At the expiration of said thirty days, the assessment roll shall be placed in the hands of the Collector, with a warrant, in the usual form, but returnable in sixty days, directing him to collect the sums unpaid thereon, and five per cent in addition, to defray the cost of collection, and one per cent per month on the amount of each assessment, from the time he received the rolls to the time when the same is paid or collected. The City Collector, at the expiration of said sixty days, shall make due return to the Receiver of Taxes of his doings under said warrant. If any portion of the assessment or tax remains due or unpaid, it shall be the duty of the Receiver of Taxes to proceed and sell the real estate upon which the assessment shall be a lien, in the manner prescribed in chapter twenty five of the Revised Ordinances of 1863.

SEC. 10. The proceeds of each special assessment levied for the building of walks aforesaid, shall be paid to the contractor to whom the same may be due upon the warrant of the Controller, as soon as the same shall be collected : *Provided*, That no money shall be so paid until the work for which it was assessed and collected shall be completed to the satisfaction of the Street Commissioner.

SEC. 11. All sidewalks in the City of Detroit shall be kept in good repair by the owner, agent or occupant of the house, lot or premises adjoining or fronting on such, and whenever any sidewalk within the limits of said City shall require repairing, it shall be the duty of the Street Commissioner of the district in which the same is situated, whenever directed by the Common Council or any Alderman, to notify by a written or printed, or a partly written and partly printed notice, the owner, agent or occupant of such house, lot or other premises adjacent to or fronting on such parts of said sidewalk, needing such repairs, to repair the same within forty-eight hours, and if the person thus notified shall refuse or neglect to comply with the exigency of said notice, then the said Street Commissioner shall have said repairs made, and shall report the making of the same, together with a detailed statement of the cost of making said repairs to the City Surveyor, who shall prepare and transmit to the Common Council a proper assessment roll, assessing the expense of said repairs upon said lot or premises, which roll shall be confirmed and collected by the Common Council in the same manner as hereinbefore provided for constructing sidewalks.

SEC. 12. If any lot or premises in front of or adjacent to which any sidewalk is ordered to be built or repaired shall be unoccupied, and the owner, agent or occupant thereof cannot be found in the City of Detroit, said Street Commissioner may serve said notice by posting the same in some conspicuous position upon said lot or premises.

SEC. 13. In case any owner, agent or occupant shall neglect to build or repair any sidewalk within the time prescribed in the notice of the Street Commissioner, as provided in this Ordinance, such owner, agent or occupant shall be liable to the City of Detroit for all damages which shall be recovered against the City for any accidents or injuries occurring by reason of such neglect, and also to prosecution in the Recorder's Court, and on conviction thereof, to a fine not exceeding fifty dollars. And if the Street Commissioner neglect, when required, to give such notice, or to have such walk built or repaired, within a reasonable time after he is so directed, he shall also be liable to similar prosecution and fine; and in the imposition of such fine in either case, the Court may make a further sentence that the offender be imprisoned in the Detroit House of Correction for any period of time not exceeding three months, or until such fine be paid. Any violation of any of the provisions of this Ordinance shall, upon conviction of the offense in the Recorder's Court, be punished by a fine not exceeding one hundred dollars, and, in the imposition of such fine, the

Court may make a further sentence that the offender be imprisoned in the Detroit House of Correction for a period of time not exceeding three months, or until such fine be paid.

SEC. 14. The Common Council shall have power to provide, by resolution, the mode of receiving proposals and entering into contracts for building and repairing all sidewalks constructed or repaired under this Ordinance.

CHAPTER 37.

THE USE OF STREETS AND ALLEYS.

[Chapter Twenty-nine of the Revised Ordinances of 1863.]

SECTION 1. No person shall permit any snow or ice to remain on the sidewalk in front, side or rear of any house, premises, building or lot occupied by him or her, or sidewalk in front, on the side or rear of any unoccupied or vacant house, premises, building or lot owned by him or her, or for which he or she is agent, lessee, administrator, administratrix or guardian, or of which he or she has charge or control for any purpose whatever, longer than twenty-four hours after the same has fallen or formed. And when ice is formed on any sidewalk as aforesaid, such occupant, owner, agent, lessee, administrator, administratrix, guardian or person or persons having charge or control thereof, as above provided, shall, within four hours after the same has formed, cause a sufficient quantity of salt, sawdust, sand or ashes to be strewn on the sidewalk, as aforesaid, in such manner as will render it safe for persons walking thereon. [*As amended by Ordinance approved December 28, 1868.*]

SEC. 2. No person shall remove or cause to be removed, or aid or assist in removing any building into, along or across any street, alley or other public space, without permission first obtained from the Common Council; in granting which permission the Council shall designate the route to be taken and the time to be occupied in the removal of such building, and such building or any bulky article, while in transit, shall be moved so as to least obstruct the street, and by the route, and in the time prescribed by the Common Council. Nor shall any person leave a building or any bulky article in any street-crossing. Any person obtaining such permission shall file a bond to the satisfaction of the Controller, conditioned that he will pay all damages to public or private property that shall be caused by removing buildings or bulky articles. The Superintendent of Police shall ascertain that any person moving a building, as aforesaid, shall have the proper permission therefor, and in case it is found that permission has not been granted, it shall be the duty of the Police to at once make the proper complaint. [*As amended by Ordinance approved January 6, 1871.*]

SEC. 3. No person shall drive, lead or back any horse, mule, ox, cow, or other animal, or team, cart or wheel carriage, on any sidewalk.

SEC. 4. No person, owning, building, or repairing any house or other building, shall permit any lumber, brick, plaster, mortar, earth, clay, sand, stone, or other material, to remain on the sidewalk after sunset of the day upon which it was placed there, without the permission of the Mayor, Common Council, or Street Commissioner.

SEC. 5. No person shall obstruct or encumber any public wharf, street or alley, or other public space, with any article or thing whatsoever. This section shall not be construed to prohibit merchants and other business persons from using and occupying the side of the sidewalks next to their places of business, for a distance of three feet, for the purpose of displaying their goods and wares, or merchandise; nor to prohibit them from using five feet of the outside of all walks twenty feet in width; nor shall it be construed to prevent the moving of goods, wares or merchandise across any sidewalk in the way of trade, or for the use of families. [*As amended by Ordinance approved January 6, 1871.*]

SEC. 6. No person shall leave any wagon, cart, carriage, sleigh, or other vehicle, standing in any street, alley or public space, without the same is actually in use at the time.

SEC. 7. No person shall place, by himself or another, any stone, timber, lumber, planks, boards, bricks or other materials, in, or upon any street, alley or other public space, except for the purpose of building, and not for that purpose, except under permission first obtained from the Mayor, Common Council, or the Street Commissioner; and such material shall not be allowed to remain in such street, alley, or other public space, after the completion of such building, or for a longer period than four months, and the same shall not be allowed to occupy and obstruct more than one-half of any street or alley; and after such building has been completed, all building material, dirt and rubbish arising therefrom, shall be removed.

SEC. 8. No person shall leave any horse, mule, oxen, or team, in any street, alley or public space, without being sufficiently tied; and no person shall halt any wagon, cart, carriage, sleigh, or other vehicle, on any cross-walk or footway.

SEC. 9. No person shall make or construct any drain or sewer, in any street or other public space, within four feet of the curb-stone of the side-walk, unless it be the drain or sewer leading to or from the building or lot for which the same is designed.

SEC. 10. No person shall dig or tear up any pavement, side or cross-walk, or dig any hole, ditch, drain or sewer in any street, alley or other public space, without permission first obtained from the Mayor, Common Council or Street Commissioner; and it shall be the duty of any person, digging or tearing up any pavement, side or cross-walk, or digging any hole, ditch, drain, or sewer, in any street, alley or other public space, as speedily as practicable to repair and put the same in as good order and condition as before; and in order to do this, such person shall pound down the earth so as to make it firm and solid; and if the earth shall settle, such person shall fill the same, from time to time, as may be necessary; and any person digging in any street, alley or other public space, or the contractor or owner or owners of property for whose benefit such digging may be done, for any of the purposes hereinbefore mentioned or for any purpose whatever, shall erect and maintain a good and sufficient fence, railing or barrier around such excavation, in such a manner as to prevent accidents, and to place and keep upon such railing, fence or barrier, suitable and sufficient colored lights during the night. [*As Amended by Ordinance approved December 12, 1870.*]

SEC. 11. No person shall herd together, or detain in any street, alley, or other public space, any cattle, horses, hogs, sheep or goats.

SEC. 12. No person shall place or put any trough for feeding or watering horses, cattle, or other animals, in any street, alley or other public space.

SEC. 13. No person shall keep or maintain on any sidewalk, any wagon or stand for the sale of goods, wares or merchandise, vegetables or fruits, to project more than three feet from the wall of his or her house or store.

SEC. 14. No person shall display or detain for exhibition any stud-horse or bull in any street, alley or other public space. [*As amended by Ordinance approved June 1, 1866.*]

SEC. 15. No person shall ride or drive any horse, carriage, sleigh or other vehicle, through any street or avenue in this City, at a faster rate than six miles per hour: *Provided,* That the prohibition in this section contained shall not be construed to apply to the driving of sleighs in an easterly direction on Lafayette avenue, Howard street, on Jefferson avenue east of Chene street, and in a southerly direction on Cass avenue, between the hours of three and five o'clock P. M. of any day, except Sunday. [*As amended by Ordinance approved January 6, 1871.*]

SEC. 16. No person shall erect any balustrade or balcony, to extend beyond the line of any sidewalk or street, and less than twelve feet from the ground, without permission first obtained from the Common Council; and iron braces and railings shall be used in the construction of any such balustrades or balconies, and the same shall not project beyond the line of the sidewalk more than three feet.

SEC. 17. No person shall play any game of nine or ten pins, ball, wicket or other games, in any street, alley or other public space.

SEC. 18. It shall not be lawful to gather in crowds on any sidewalk or in any street, so as to obstruct travel therein, or encumber the same.

SEC. 19. Every owner or occupant of a lot, where the same is used for business purposes, having a store, office, lumber yard, mill, factory, etc., thereon, shall erect in front of the same a hitching post, or in cases where there is a stone pavement a substantial iron ring in lieu thereof, may be firmly fixed in the outer edge of said pavement. [*As amended by Ordinance approved August 2, 1867.*]

SEC. 20. No wooden post for the purpose of supporting any awning, shall be erected or set up in any paved street, avenue or public space, and all iron posts erected in any paved street, avenue or other public space, for the purpose of supporting awnings, shall be not less than eight feet in height, and to be placed next to and alongside the curbstone; and no rails or strips of boards shall be used to connect such posts with the buildings.

SEC. 21. No awning, or cloth or canvas used as an awning, shall be permitted to hang within eight feet of the sidewalk.

SEC. 22. No person shall suspend from any house, shop or store, into or over any street, alley or other public space, any lamp, sign, goods, clothes, wares or other article or substance, so that the same shall extend or project from the wall or front of such building more than three feet.

SEC. 23. No person shall make or continue any cellar door, windows or area, so that the same shall extend more than four feet beyond the line of any sidewalk; and all areas shall be protected by sufficient grating or illuminated pavement.

SEC. 24. Every entrance or flight of steps projecting beyond the line of the sidewalk, and descending into any cellar or basement story, where such entrance or flight of steps shall not be covered, shall be enclosed with a good iron railing on each side, permanently put up, not less than three feet high, with a gate opening inwardly, unless such entrance steps be thoroughly lighted, so as to prevent accidents; and such steps and railing shall not occupy more than one-fifth of the width of the sidewalk.

SEC. 25. No person shall construct or continue any porch over a cellar door so that the same shall project beyond the line of any alley or other public space.

SEC. 26. No person shall dig or construct, or cause to be dug or constructed, any area to or around any cellar or basement story, so that the same shall extend more than four feet beyond the line of any sidewalk; and no vault shall be dug or constructed to extend beyond the curb line of the street.

SEC. 27. No person shall swim or bathe in any of the waters in or adjoining the City of Detroit, so as to be exposed to the view of spectators.

SEC. 28. No person shall hoist or raise from any street into any building, loft, store or room, or lower from any building, store, loft or room into any street, any cask, bale, bundle, box, crate, or any goods, wares or merchandise, boards, joists, timber, or article whatever, by means of any rope, pulley, tackle or windlass.

SEC. 29. Any cellar or other excavation left uncovered by the burning or removal of the buildings therefrom, shall be surrounded, by the owner or occupant of the premises, with a sufficient fence or barrier to prevent accidents. [*Added by Ordinance approved December 30, 1870.*]

SEC. 30. Any violations of the provisions of this Ordinance shall be punished by a fine not to exceed one hundred dollars and costs of prosecution, and the offender may be imprisoned in the Detroit House of Correction until the payment thereof: *Provided, however,* That the term of such imprisonment shall not exceed six months.

SEC. 31. It is hereby made the duty of the members of the Metropolitan Police and Street Commissioners of the City, to see that the provisions of this Ordinance are faithfully observed, and to make complaint for all violations of the same.

[Chapter Thirty-seven of the Revised Ordinances of 1863, as amended.]

SEC. 32. It shall be the duty of the City Attorney, or other legal adviser of the Corporation, to insert in all contracts for paving or grading streets, avenues, lanes, or alleys, or for constructing sewers, drains, or reservoirs, or for doing any work whatever, whereby accidents or injuries may occur in consequence of any neglect or carelessness on the part of the contractor, a covenant requiring the contractor to place and maintain the fences, railing, or barriers, in the manner provided for in Section 10 of this Chapter, for the prevention of accidents, and keep and save the City harmless and indemnified against all loss and damage, which may be occasioned by reason of any negligence or carlessness in the manner of doing such work.

SEC. 33. In all cases where any person or persons shall perform any work, as provided in the preceding section, either under contracts with the Corporation, or by virtue of any permission from the Common Council, or any department or officer of the City, such person shall be liable to the City of Detroit for any and every loss or damage which said Corporation may sustain, and for all sums which it may have to pay to any person or persons, by reason of any loss or injury sustained in consequence of any carelessness or negligence in doing the work, or by reason of any neglect or failure to comply with the provisions of this Ordinance.

SEC. 34. Any person performing work, as provided in this Ordinance, who shall neglect or refuse to comply with its provisions, shall be punished by a fine not to exceed one hundred dollars and costs; and in the imposition of any such fine and costs, the court may make a further sentence, that the offender may be imprisoned in the Detroit House of Correction until the payment thereof, for any period of time not exceeding six months.

CHAPTER 38.

COLLECTION OF BENEFITS AND COSTS IN OPENING ALLEYS.

[Ordinance approved September 1, 1870.]

SECTION 1. The amounts of money apportioned to and assessed upon any lot or lots of land, premises or subdivisions thereof, in proceedings had or taken for the opening of any alley, for the benefits accrued and assessed upon any such property prior to the 5th day of April, A. D. 1869, and not paid into the treasury, as provided in Section 28 of Chapter 7 of the City Charter of 1857, shall be collected in the same manner, and the same proceedings shall be adopted and taken for the collection of the same, with the interest and charges, and for advertising, selling and conveying and for redemption after sale, as are provided by the Charter and Ordinances for collection of assessments to pay the cost and expense of paving streets.

SEC. 2. In case of assessment upon any lot or lots, or subdivisions thereof, for the benefit of opening any alley, which shall have been assessed since the 5th day of April, A. D. 1869, the Receiver of Taxes, after the prior proceedings provided by Section 25 of Chapter 7 of the City Charter of 1857, as amended by act of the Legislature, approved April 5, 1869, shall have been taken, shall immediately proceed in the manner provided in the City Charter and Ordinances in cases of special assessments for paving streets, to advertise and sell such parts and parcels of the property assessed as shall not have been discharged of such assessment by payment, and shall take such subsequent proceedings thereupon, in every respect, as are provided by the Charter and Ordinances in case of unpaid special assessments for street paving.

SEC. 3. All moneys collected under this Ordinance shall be paid into the City Treasury, to the credit of the Contingent Fund.

CHAPTER 39.

PUBLIC PARKS AND PLACES.

[Chapter Thirty-five of the Revised Ordinances of 1863.]

SECTION 1. No person shall place any building, or obstruction of any kind, on a public park or space.

SEC. 2. No person shall take down, climb over, interfere with, disturb or displace any rails, posts, boards, chains or fences, enclosing any public park or space.

SEC. 3. No person shall play at any game, or sport, in any enclosed public park or space.

SEC. 4. No person shall climb, peel, cut, deface, remove, injure or destroy any tree, in any public park or space.

SEC. 5. No person shall stand, walk, or lie upon any part of a public park or space, laid out and appropriated for grass or shrubbery.

SEC. 6. No person shall pluck, break, trample upon, or interfere with any flower or shrub, in any public park or space.

SEC. 7. No person shall dig, remove, or carry away any sward, gravel, sand, turf or earth, in any public park or space.

SEC. 8. No person shall place or deposit any dead carcass, ordure, filth, dirt, stones, or other matter or substance, on any public park or space.

SEC. 9. No person shall hang, post, place, or put any bill, notice, sign, placard, carpet, or other incumbrance on any tree, fountain, post, railing, fence, or other erection, in or surrounding any public park or space.

SEC. 10. No person shall wade into, or throw any wood, sand, stone, or other substance, into any basin, pool or fountain, in any public park or space.

SEC. 11. No person shall molest, or in any manner disturb or annoy the fish, or other animals, which may be placed in any fountain, pool or basin, in any public park or space.

SEC. 12. The person or persons in charge of the public parks or spaces, shall have and possess the powers of policemen, and it is hereby made the duty of such person or persons, to observe that the provisions of this Ordinance are strictly complied with, and to make complaint to the Recorder's Court, for any violation of its provisions.

SEC. 13. Any violation of the provisions of this Ordinance shall be punished by a fine not to exceed one hundred dollars, and costs; and in the imposition of any fine and costs, the Court may make a further sentence, that the offender be imprisoned in the County Jail, or in the Detroit House of Correction, until such fine and costs be paid: *Provided, however*, that the term of such imprisonment shall not exceed the period of six months.

CHAPTER 40.

WHARVES.

[Chapter Forty-four of the Revised Ordinances of 1863.]

SECTION 1. It shall be the duty of the owner or owners, occupant or occupants, lessee or lessees, of any of the wharves of this City, bordering upon the Detroit River, and which are not fenced in, or otherwise enclosed, so as to prevent the passage of travelers or others over or across them, to keep the same in good order and condition, and whenever any of the plank, boards, timber or other materials composing or forming a part of any of the wharves of said City, shall, from any cause, become loose, or be removed, or whenever any of said wharves shall in any manner, and from any cause whatever, be out of repair, it shall be the duty of the members of the Metropolitan Police to notify either the owner or owners, occupant or occupants, lessee or lessees, of any such wharf or wharves, to immediately replace and securely fasten the plank, board, or other material so removed as aforesaid, or otherwise to repair such wharf or wharves as may seem necessary: *Provided*, That the notice so to be given may be either a verbal or written notice, and may be given by the Mayor or any of the Aldermen, or other officers of the City; and if a written notice, it may be either served personally upon, or left at the place of business or residence of the person or persons notified.

SEC. 2. In case the person or persons so notified, as provided for in the preceding section, shall neglect for twenty-four hours after such notice, to comply with the requisitions thereof, he, she or they shall, on conviction thereof before the Recorder's Court, be liable to a fine of not less than five, nor more than fifty dollars for each and every day he, she or they shall neglect to comply with the requisitions of said notice.

CHAPTER 41.

NUMBERING OF BUILDINGS.

[Ordinance approved June 10, 1869.]

SECTION 1. All dwelling-houses or other buildings erected or fronting on any street, lane, alley or public court within the City of Detroit, shall be numbered, in the manner as hereinafter prescribed.

SEC. 2. The numbering of said dwelling-houses or other buildings, as aforesaid, shall be in accordance with the plan prepared by Eugene Robinson, Esq., filed in the City Clerk's office on the tenth day of June, A. D. 1868; and the books containing said plan shall be a public record, and shall be open for inspection at all times, and accessible to all persons.

SEC. 3. The Common Council may designate and appoint some competent person or persons to affix numbers, as hereinafter provided, in accordance with the plan filed as aforesaid, on all dwellings or other buildings, as above prescribed: *Provided, however*, That the owner or agent in any capacity of any building or premises, upon receiving notice, as hereinafter provided, and complying with the requirements of this Ordinance, may affix or inscribe the proper number or numbers to said building or premises, without interference in any manner from the person or persons appointed as aforesaid.

SEC. 4. Whenever any building or premises, as aforesaid, shall be without a number or numbers, or shall have the wrong number affixed or inscribed thereon, it shall be the duty of the members of the Metropolitan Police to serve or cause to be served on the owner or agent, as aforesaid, a written or printed notice notifying said owner or agent to affix or inscribe, within ten days from the date of the service of such notice, on the building or premises owned by him or her, or for which he or she may be the agent in any capacity, the proper number or numbers, as designated in said notice; and it shall be the duty of such owner or agent to affix or inscribe the number or numbers so designated, in plain and legible figures, in a conspicuous place on the front of said building or premises. Such notice shall be served personally on such owner or agent, or by leaving the same at the residence of such owner or agent, or, in case they or their residence cannot be found, the same shall be served on any occupant of the premises, and if the same are unoccupied, by posting said notice in some conspicuous place upon the premises. The officer serving said notice shall report in writing once in each week to the City Clerk any neglect or refusal on the part of persons so notified to comply with the provisions of this Ordinance.

SEC. 5. In case of refusal or neglect to affix or inscribe the number or numbers so designated within the time limited in said notice, the person or persons appointed by the Common Council, as aforesaid, shall affix said number or numbers, and receive therefor, for each number furnished or affixed, such compensation as the Common Council shall prescribe.

SEC. 6. Any owner or agent, as aforesaid, neglecting to affix or inscribe the number or numbers in the manner above provided, after due notice, as aforesaid, who shall refuse to have his or her premises or buildings so numbered by the person or persons authorized by the Common Council, shall for every such offense, on conviction before the Recorder's Court, forfeit the sum of five dollars and costs of prosecution.

SEC. 7. The cost of numbering the building or premises, as aforesaid, by the person or persons appointed, as aforesaid, by the Common Council, shall be paid by the owner or agent of the buildings or premises so numbered, and shall be a lien upon the lots or lands upon which the building or buildings are situated, and shall be collected in the same manner as for unpaid special assessments.

SEC. 8. The person or persons appointed by the Common Council to affix the numbers, as aforesaid, before entering upon the duties of the office, shall execute a bond to the City of Detroit in the penal sum of five hundred dollars, with two sureties, conditioned for the faithful performance of the work.

SEC. 9. Any person or persons not duly authorized to perform the services aforesaid, who shall assume to be authorized, and shall attempt to affix any number or numbers to buildings or premises, as aforesaid, shall, for every such offense, on conviction before the Recorder's Court, forfeit a penalty of not less than three dollars nor more than twenty-five dollars.

CHAPTER 42.

WIDTH OF STREETS.

[Ordinance Approved August 2, 1867.]

SECTION 1. Hereafter all streets which shall be opened or recorded in the City limits shall be of a width of at least fifty feet.

[Ordinance approved October 4, 1866.]

SEC. 2. That the roadway on State street, from the west line of Rowland street to the east line of Cass street, be, and the same is hereby established at a width of thirty-two feet.

[Ordinance approved May 27, 1870.]

SEC. 3. That the roadway on Duffield street from the east line Cass avenue to the west line of Woodward avenue, be, and the same is hereby established at a width of twenty-four feet.

CHAPTER 43.

FOOT OF ORLEANS STREET.

[Ordinance approved November 23, 1870.]

Whereas, The Board of Water Commissioners is now engaged in the erection of a new engine house, in which a new engine is being set up, and making other extensive and necessary improvements in the hydraulic yard, adjoining Orleans street, in the City of Detroit, which, in consequence of the limited room in the yard, they are unable to accomplish without being permitted to occupy for a limited time, a portion of said street.

Therefore, It is hereby ordained by the Common Council of the City of Detroit:

SECTION 1. That permission is hereby given to said Board of Commissioners to use the westerly half of said street, from the southerly line of the dock thereof, running back two hundred feet, for placing thereon the material or other property which may be required for any of the purposes aforesaid, embracing such cordwood as may be required for the use of the works, until said erections and improvements are completed, not to exceed four months from the date hereof, any Ordinance or usage to the contrary notwithstanding.

CHAPTER 44.

IMPROVEMENT OF WASHINGTON AVENUE.

[Chapter Forty of the Revised Ordinances of 1863.]

SECTION 1. The width of the wagon way on Washington avenue shall be forty feet from curb to curb, running through the central portion of said avenue.

SEC. 2. The width of the grass plat on each side of the wagon way shall be twenty-four feet.

SEC. 3. The width of the sidewalks on said avenue shall be sixteen feet, running parallel to and adjoining said grass plat.

SEC. 4. The said grass plat of twenty-four feet shall be ornamented with two rows of shade trees; one to be placed two feet from the curb-stone, and the other two feet from the sidewalk on each side of said wagon way. The trees shall not be less than twenty feet apart, and shall be protected by suitable guard boxes of a uniform pattern and size.

SEC. 5. Said wagon way shall be paved or graveled, under the direction of the Street Commissioner for the Western District, according to the adopted plans and specifications for paving for the year 1860.

SEC. 6. The remaining portions of said avenue on each side thereof, and between said sidewalks and the line of said avenue, shall be improved and ornamented by turfing and planting ornamental trees and shrubbery. Said ornamental grounds shall be protected by a suitable iron fence or railing.

SEC. 7. The said grass plat of twenty-four feet shall be subdrained with suitable tile drains, in accordance with the plan hitherto submitted, and the entire of said improvements on said avenue, to wit: the paving or graveling, grading, turfing, subdraining, planting of trees, boxing the same, and the fencing or railing, shall be done by the property owners on said avenue without any expense to the City, and the said improvements shall at all times be kept in good and substantial repair by the said property owners, at their own expense and costs: *Provided, however*, that if said improvements are not made and completed within eighteen months from the passage of this Ordinance, and if there shall, at any time, be any neglect on the part of said property owners, their heirs and assignees, to keep said improvements in good order and repair, or if they in any way neglect to comply with the provisions of this Ordinance, no rights or privileges shall accrue to said property owners on said avenue; but all such rights and privileges under this Ordinance shall cease at the election of the City.

SEC. 8. The entire ornamental grounds on said avenue shall at all times be under the supervision of the Common Council, through their Committee on Parks.

SEC. 9. Unless the property holders upon Washington Grand avenue shall, within thirty days from the taking effect of this Ordinance, file their written assent to the same in the office of the City Clerk, the said Ordinance and all its provisions shall cease and become inoperative and of no effect.

SEC. 10. All Ordinances or parts of Ordinances conflicting with this Ordinance are hereby repealed: *Provided*, That nothing in this Ordinance contained, shall be construed in a manner to affect the existing legal rights of the City in and to the enclosed portions of said street.

CHAPTER 45.

IMPROVEMENT OF ALEXANDRINE AVENUE.

[Ordinance Approved November 17, 1865.]

SECTION 1. Two sidewalks are hereby authorized and directed to be constructed and laid upon Alexandrine avenue, in said city —one upon the southerly and one upon the northerly side of said avenue, and extending from Woodward avenue to Cass street. Each of said walks shall be of the width of six feet, and shall be located so that their outside lines will be distant three feet from the curb stones of said avenue on the respective sides on which such walks are laid. The three feet lying between such walks and curbs may be used for ornamental purposes.

SEC. 2. Such walks shall be laid and constructed in conformity with the provisions of the Ordinances of the City.

CHAPTER 46.

TO VACATE CAMPUS MARTIUS.

[Chapter Forty-one of the Revised Ordinances of 1863.]

SECTION 1. All that portion of the public grounds in the City of Detroit, known and described as the *Campus Martius*, lying west of Woodward avenue and between Michigan avenue and Fort street, in this City, shall be, and the same is hereby discontinued and vacated as public ground, for the following purposes, and no other, to wit: For the purpose of using and occupying the same as a site for the erection and use of a building, and the necessary appurtenances, to be known as the City Hall, and to be used for the purposes of a hall for the sessions of the Common Council, City Courts, and such other Courts as the City authorities may see fit to allow; City offices and such other public offices as the said authorities may see fit to allow to be kept therein; and for any other objects or purposes connected with the interests of said City, the County of Wayne, or the State of Michigan, which said authorities may, from time to time, see fit to countenance and permit.

CHAPTER 47.

LAMPS AND LAMP POSTS.

[Chapter Thirty-four of the Revised Ordinances of 1863.]

SECTION 1. The public lamps and lamp posts in the City shall be under the supervision of the Inspector of Gas Meters.

SEC. 2. No person shall willfully, maliciously, or negligently injure, pull down, break, remove, or in any manner deface, or injure any public lamp, lamp post, crotchet, or gas light, within the City of Detroit.

SEC. 3. No person shall light, or cause to be lighted, or extinguish, or cause to be extinguished, any public lamp or gas light, without being authorized so to do, either by the Common Council, the Mayor, Controller, Inspector of Gas Meters, or the Detroit Gas Light Company.

SEC. 4. No person shall hang or place any article or substance whatever upon, or place any box, or other heavy material, against, or hitch any horse, or other animal, to any public lamp or lamp post, in this City.

SEC. 5. No person shall erect, place or suspend any lamp or lamp post, in any public street, lane or alley, in this City, without permission from the Common Council.

SEC. 6. Any violation of the provisions of this Ordinance shall be punished by a fine not to exceed the sum of twenty-five dollars and costs, and in the imposition of any fine and costs, the Court may make a further sentence, that the offender be imprisoned in the Detroit House of Correction until the payment thereof, for any term not exceeding six months.

TITLE IV.

STREET RAILWAYS, RAILROADS, STEAMBOATS AND VESSELS.

CHAPTER 48.

DETROIT CITY RAILWAY COMPANY.

[Chapter Ninety-three of the Revised Ordinances of 1863.]

Whereas, Cornelius S. Bushnell, John A. Griswold, Nehemiah D. Sperry, Eben N. Willcox, their associates, successors and assigns, propose to organize, as a body, politic and corporate, under a Charter from the Legislature of Michigan, or under the "Act to provide for the construction of Tram Railways," approved February 13th, 1855 (Laws of 1855, page 338), and act or acts amendatory thereto, for the purpose of constructing and operating in and through the streets of the City of Detroit, City or Street Railways; therefore, *Be it ordained by the Common Council of the City of Detroit:*

SECTION 1. That consent, permission and authority is hereby given, granted, and duly vested in Eben N. Willcox, and his associates, who may be approved by the Council, their successors and assigns, organized into a Corporation, under the laws of the State of Michigan, as aforesaid, to lay a single or double track for a Railway, with all the necessary and convenient tracks for turnouts, side tracks and switches, in and along the course of the streets of, and bridges in, the City of Detroit, hereinafter mentioned, and the same to keep, maintain and use, and to operate thereon Railway Cars and Carriages, during all the term hereinfter specified and prescribed, and in the manner, and upon the condition set forth in this Ordinance.

SEC. 2. The said grantees are, by the provisions of this Ordinance, exclusively authorized to construct and operate Railways, as herein provided, on and through Jefferson, Michigan and Woodward avenues, Witherell, Gratiot, Grand River, and Brush or Beaubien streets; and from Jefferson avenue, through Brush or Beaubien streets, to Atwater street; and from Jefferson avenue, at its intersection with Woodbridge street, to Third street; up Third street, to Fort street; and through Fort street, to the western limits of the City; and through such other streets and avenues, in said City, as may, from time to time, be fixed and determined by vote of the Common Council of the said City of Detroit, and assented to, in writing, by said Corporation, organized as provided in section first of this Ordinance: *And provided,* The Corporation does not assent, in writing, within thirty days after the passage of said resolution of the Council, ordering the formation of new routes, then the Common Council may give the privilege to any other Company to build such route, and such other Company shall have the right to cross any track of rails already laid, at their own cost and expense: *Provided, always,* That the Railways on Grand River street, Gratiot street, and Michigan avenue, shall each run into and connect with the Woodward avenue Railways, in such direction that said Railways shall be continued down to, and form, each of them, one continuous route to Jefferson avenue: *Provided, always,* That said Railroad down Gratiot street may be continued to Woodward avenue, through State street, or through Randolph street, and Monroe avenue and the Campus Martius, as the grantees or their assigns, under this Ordinance, may elect.

SEC. 3. The Railways through all the streets shall be laid in the centre thereof, if on a single track, and if on a double track, the inside rail of each track shall be laid a sufficient distance from the centre of the street, to enable two cars to pass on opposite tracks, and leave a space between of at least eighteen inches, and the gauge of the track shall be at least four feet eight and one-half inches, and so as to accommodate the most common width of carriage wheels: *Provided, however,*

That where a double track shall not be laid in the first instance, and a second track shall afterwards be required, such second track may be laid upon either side of the first: *And provided further*, That in all streets which are not paved, or where plank roads are laid, the tracks of said Railways may be laid elsewhere than in the centre thereof, as may be most convenient, under the direction of the Common Council, and shall least obstruct the public travel thereon. When the grantees shall complete one track of the said Railway, and place cars thereon for public use, they may at any time thereafter, within five years, build a second track, so that they do not interrupt the running of their cars on the first completed track; *Provided*, The consent of the Common Council is first obtained.

SEC. 4. The track of said railways shall be laid of such rails as shall least obstruct the free passage of vehicles or carriages over the same; and the upper surface of the rails shall be laid flush with the surface of the streets, and shall conform to the grades thereof, as now established, or as they shall, from time to time, be re-established or altered; and in case of grading, paving, or otherwise, if it be necessary to relay said rails, the same shall be done at the expense of the grantees; and in all streets, or parts of streets, which are not paved, the rails shall be laid in such manner as shall least interfere with the public travel thereon, and as shall be authorized and approved by the City Surveyor. The grantees, and their assigns, shall be required to keep the surface of the streets, inside the rails, and for two feet four inches outside thereof, in good order and repair, and all snow, ice, dirt and filth, cleared and removed from the same, at the expense of the grantees: *Provided, however*, That upon the paved portions of said streets, the materials for repaving shall be supplied at the expense of the City.

SEC. 5. The routes of all said railways shall commence in the Woodward avenue road, at Campus Martius; from thence running on their several courses, to the outer limits of the City: *Provided*, That in collecting fare, those portions between Atwater, through Brush or Beaubien streets, and through Woodward avenue to Jefferson avenue, and between Brush or Beaubien and Third streets, on Jefferson avenue and Woodbridge street, shall be respectively deemed to belong to either of the above routes, any portion of which is then being traveled continuously by any one passenger at the same time, shall pay only one fare.

SEC. 6. Said railway on Woodward avenue, or Witherell street, to Park lot sixty-two, through Jefferson avenue to the eastern limits, and through Jefferson avenue to Woodbridge, through Woodbridge to Third, and up Third to Fort, and through Fort street to the western limits of the City, shall be completed within six months from the thirty-first day of March, A. D. 1863, and through Gratiot street to the easterly line of the B. Chapaton farm, shall be completed within three years from and after the thirty-first day of March A. D. 1863; and through Grand River street to the easterly line of the Woodbridge farm; through Michigan avenue to Thompson street, shall be completed to within two years from and after the thirty-first day of March, A. D. 1863; and the remainder thereof, at such times as the public necessity may require: *Provided*, That no such railway shall be required to be laid through any part of such routes, which shall not be worked up to the established grade thereof, until the City shall have completed such work.

SEC. 7. The cars to be used on said railways shall be drawn by animals only, at a speed not exceeding the rate of six miles per hour, and shall be run as often as public convenience shall require, and the Common Council shall prescribe: *Provided always*, That said Council will not require them to run regular cars oftener than once in twenty minutes during fourteen hours every day, from the fifteenth day of April to the fifteenth day of October, and twelve hours every day from the fifteenth day of October to the fifteenth day of April, and the cars in use upon said Railways shall be run for no other purpose than to transport passengers and their ordinary baggage, and the cars and carriages for that purpose shall be of the best style in use on such Railways: *Provided*, That other cars and carriages may be used for cleaning said railway tracks from obstructions by snow, or otherwise.

SEC. 8. The rate of fare for any distance shall not exceed five cents in any one car, or on any one route named in this Ordinance, except where cars or carriages shall be chartered for specific purposes: *Provided,* Cars so chartered shall not be considered regular cars, within the meaning of the preceding section.

Sec. 9. Cars drawn in the same direction shall not approach each other within a distance of one hundred feet, except in cases of accident or at stations, or for the purpose of connecting two cars together.

Sec. 10. No car shall be allowed to stop on a cross-walk, or in front of any intersecting street, except to avoid collision or prevent danger to persons or property in the street.

Sec. 11. When the conductor of any car is required to stop at the intersection of streets, to receive or leave passengers, the cars shall be stopped so as to leave the rear platform slightly over the crossing.

Sec. 12. The grantees, or their assigns, shall employ careful, sober, and prudent agents, conductors and drivers, to take charge of their cars while on the road, and it shall be the duty of all such agents, conductors, and drivers, to keep vigilant watch for all trains, carriages, or persons on foot, and especially children, either upon the track or moving towards it; at the first appearance of danger to such teams, carriages, footmen, or children, or other obstructions, the cars shall be stopped in the shortest time and space possible.

Sec. 13. Conductors shall not allow ladies or children to enter or leave the cars while in motion.

Sec. 14. Conductors shall announce to the passengers the names of the principal squares and streets, as the cars reach them.

Sec. 15. The cars shall, at all times, be entitled to the track, and any vehicles upon the track of said railways, shall turn out when any car comes up, so as to leave the track unobstructed, and the drivers of any vehicle refusing to do so, shall be liable to a fine not exceeding five dollars, on conviction before the Recorder's Court, of said City of Detroit; and costs of prosecution shall not be at the expense of the City.

Sec. 16. The cars, after sunset, shall be provided with colored signal lights, a red light in front, and a green light in rear.

Sec. 17. Wherever gas or water pipes, or sewers, are now laid in the streets herein specified, and through which railways are to pass, the said railways must be laid down and maintained subject to the right now in the City, and the Gas Company, and the Sewer and Water Commissioners, to take up or remove said pipes or sewers, in such a manner as not unnecessarily to damage or injure said railways or their use, without claim against the City, Gas Company, or Water or Sewer Commissioners; and the Common Council expressly reserves to itself the right hereafter to lay down, or to permit to be laid down, and repaired in said streets, gas or water pipes, and sewers, whenever the public or private convenience may require; the said Gas or Water Companies, or private individuals, who shall take up pavements for the purposes aforesaid, being always required, as by the present City Ordinance, to restore the pavement in the streets to its former condition.

Sec. 18. If said grantees, or their assigns, shall fail to complete any of the aforesaid Railways, within the time prescribed by this Ordinance, then the rights and privileges herein granted shall be forfeited as to any and every route herein established, which is not commenced and completed in the time herein prescribed, and the City shall be entitled to take possession thereof, provided the Council does not extend the time: *Provided*, That if said grantees shall be delayed by the order or injunction of any Court, and said order or injunction shall not be obtained at the instance, or by the contrivance of said grantees, then the time of such delay shall be excluded from the time of completion prescribed in this Ordinance.

Sec. 19. It is hereby reserved to the Common Council of the City of Detroit, the right to make such further rules, orders or regulations, as may, from time to time, be deemed necessary to protect the interests, safety, welfare, or accommodation of the public, in relation to said Railways.

Sec. 20. The powers and privileges conferred by the provisions of this Ordinance, shall be limited to thirty years from and after the date of its passage.

Sec. 21. Said grantees shall, on or before the tenth day of January, A. D. 1863, deposit with the Controller of said City the sum of five thousand dollars in money, or in United States stocks, or in Treasury notes, bearing seven and three-tenths per cent interest, which deposit shall be security for the completion, by said grantees, of the lines of Railway which they are required to construct and complete, on or before the first day of October, A. D. 1863; and if these said Railways shall not then be completed, the sum so deposited shall be forfeited to the City: *Provided, however*, That if said grantees, or their assigns, cannot procure the requisite amount of rail of the Philadelphia, or other suitable pattern, to build said Railways, within the time specified, with a suitable and competent force, then the time shall be extended until such rail can be obtained, and laid with a suitable and competent force: *And provided further*, That the time for the completion of said roads be extended not to exceed nine months, upon good and sufficient reasons being given, that the iron rail cannot be procured.

SEC. 22. The said grantees, and their assigns, shall pay to the Treasurer of the City of Detroit, annually, fifteen dollars on each and every passenger, or other car, excepting only those cars used for cleaning the track on said roads, to be collected as a license, for the use of the City, after the term of five years from and after this date.

SEC. 23. Whenever the said grantees, their successors or assigns, shall have organized themselves into a body politic and corporate, under the said act of the Legislature of the State of Michigan, or Charter thereof, all the powers and privileges granted and conferred to and upon them, by this Ordinance, shall be given, granted and duly vested in said Corporation, without any further action, consent, permission or authority of the Common Council, whatever.

SEC. 24. All Ordinances, or parts of Ordinances, heretofore made, ordained and passed, inconsistent with the provisions of this Ordinance, are hereby repealed.

SEC. 25. Any willful violation of, or failure to comply with the provisions of this Ordinance, by said Railway Company or by any agent, conductor, driver, or any person in the employ of said Company, shall be punished by a fine not to exceed one hundred dollars and costs; and in the imposition of any such fine and costs, the Court may make a further sentence that the offender be committed to the County Jail or to the Detroit House of Correction until the payment thereof, for any period of time not exceeding six months. [*As amended by Ordinance approved March 29, 1864.*]

[Chapter Ninety-four of the Revised Ordinances of 1863.]

SEC. 26. Permission is hereby given to the Detroit Railway to build its road and track on Michigan avenue, from Woodward avenue to Fourth street, and on Gratiot steet, from Woodward avenue to Russell street, instead and in lieu of upon Third street and Fort street, as provided by the Ordinance approved November 24, 1862, and the amendments thereto (and such building on Michigan avenue and Gratiot street, together with Jefferson and Woodward avenues, shall be deemed a compliance with the condition of deposit mentioned in section twenty-one of said Ordinance).

SEC. 27. As a condition of the acceptance of this permission, the said Detroit City Railway may and shall complete its road and track on Fort street, Michigan avenue, and Gratiot street, as provided by the aforesaid Ordinances, by the first day of October, 1864; and a failure to complete the same by that time, shall be regarded as a forfeiture of the route or routes not so completed.

SEC. 28. On Woodward avenue, Gratiot street and Michigan avenue, beyond the pavement, the said railway may build its track a sufficient distance from the plank road in those streets, respectively, to leave the grade track of said plank road clear, and allow teams and vehicles to pass between said track and said plank road; and upon Michigan avenue and Gratiot street, beyond the pavement, said railway may construct its track with the "T" rail, which is used for street railways, and weighs not less than thirty-three pounds to the yard.

SEC. 29. The said railway is hereby authorized to extend its track, and run its cars, through Third street, southerly from Woodbridge street, to the dock, and to lay the said track on such part of said street, westerly of the center, as they shall agree upon with the Michigan Central Railroad Company.

SEC. 30. The tracks upon Jefferson avenue, Woodward avenue, Michigan avenue and Gratiot street, shall each be considered and run as one route, and subject its passengers to the payment of a single fare each: *Provided, however,* That all cars running north of Jefferson avenue shall run to and from Jefferson avenue, and that portion of Woodward avenue between Jefferson avenue and the routes intersecting Woodward avenue, shall be considered as making a portion of each of said routes, respectively.

SEC. 31. The Detroit City Railway, upon obtaining the consent of the owners of real estate on Elmwood avenue, or such real estate owners as are affected thereby, may, and is hereby authorized to build a track, from its present track on Jefferson avenue, to Elmwood Cemetery, and run its cars thereon at such times as will accommodate the public: *Provided, however,* No person shall be charged more than one cent either way, on this track; and said railway are also authorized to run a track and their cars to Mount Elliott Cemetery, along Mount Elliott avenue, and charge the same rate of fare as to the said Elmwood Cemetery.

[Chapter Ninety-five of the Revised Ordinances of 1863.]

SEC. 32. The Detroit City Railway is hereby authorized to build its track, and run its cars, from its track on Jefferson avenue, upon and along Randolph street southerly to Atwater street, and thence along Atwater street easterly to Brush street; and, as said track approaches the Detroit and Milwaukee depot, the said Railway may turn the same on the southerly side of said Atwater street, so as to run said cars up to the sidewalk in front of the office buildings of the Detroit and Milwaukee Railway Company.

[Ordinance approved January 4, 1864.]

SEC. 33. Permission is hereby given to the Detroit City Railway to build its road and track on and through Fort street, from Third street to Woodward avenue, instead and in lieu of on and through Third street, from Fort street to Woodbridge street, as now provided by the Ordinances regulating the building of the tracks of said Railway, in which case said Railway will be relieved of its obligations to build through Third street as aforesaid.

SEC. 34. Permission is also hereby given to said Railway to build its road and track along and through Stanton street, from Fort street to the River Road, and thence on and through the River Road to the westerly limits of the City, and such building shall relieve said Railway from its obligation to build its road and track from said Stanton street, along said Fort street, to said westerly limits of the City, and the said Railway is hereby authorized to build its track on Fort street, from the Railroad crossing, through Stanton street and River Road, to the City limits, with "T" rail, similar and of equal weight to that used on Michigan avenue.

SEC. 35. The road and track of said Railway, from said westerly limits, through said River Road, Stanton street and Fort street, and from Fort street along Woodward avenue to Jefferson avenue, shall then form one route, along which said Railway shall run its cars continuously, and on which it shall be entitled to receive one fare for each passenger.

[Ordinance approved October 8, 1864.]

SEC. 36. The Detroit City Railway Company is authorized to connect their car depot, on Second street, with their main track, by constructing a branch track from their main track to said car house, either through Second street or from Third street, through the alley, between Jefferson avenue and Front street.

SEC. 37. The time for completing the Road of said Company, on Gratiot street, is hereby extended to November 1, 1865. *Provided, however,* That said Company shall extend their track as far as Chene street, on or before the twentieth day of November next.

SEC. 38. The track of said Company shall be laid on that part of Gratiot street which is occupied by the Plank Road Company, in such position as shall be agreed on between the Railway and Plank Road Companies: *Provided, however,* That unless the line agreed on shall be along the center of said street, such agreement shall be first reported to and approved by the Council.

CHAPTER 49.

FORT STREET AND ELMWOOD AVENUE RAILWAY COMPANY.

[Ordinance passed over veto of Mayor, January 31, 1865.]

Whereas, Frederick Buhl, John P. Clark, Eber B. Ward, their associates, successors and assigns, propose to organize a body politic and corporate, under the "Act to provide for the construction of tram railways," approved February 13, 1855 (Laws of 1855, page 388), and act or acts amendatory thereto, for the purpose of constructing and operating through the streets of the City of Detroit, a city or street railway to be known as the "Fort Street and Elmwood Avenue Railway;" therefore, it is hereby ordained by the Common Council of the City of Detroit:

SECTION 1. That consent, permission and authority is hereby given, granted and duly vested in Frederick Buhl and his associates, who may be approved by the Common Council, their successors and assigns, organized into a corporation under the laws of the Sate of Michigan, as aforesaid, to lay a single or double track for a railway, with all the necessary and convenient tracks for turn-outs, side-tracks and switches, in and along the course of the streets of, and bridges in, the City of Detroit, hereinafter mentioned, and the same to keep, maintain and use and to operate thereon railway cars and carriages, during all the term hereinafter specified and prescribed, and in the manner and upon the conditions set forth in this Ordinance.

SEC. 2. The said grantees are, by the provisions of this Ordinance, authorized to construct and operate a street railway, as herein provided, upon the following route: Commencing at the present westerly limits of the City of Detroit, where Fort street touches and intersects said westerly limits; thence easterly through Fort street to Woodward avenue, and along the southerly side of Michigan avenue, to Randolph street; thence up Randolph street, and from said Randolph street to Elmwood avenue, through Croghan street the whole distance to said Elmwood avenue, provided said street can be opened without expense to the City: otherwise, through Croghan street to St. Aubin street; and thence through St. Aubin street to Clinton avenue; and thence through Clinton avenue to Elmwood avenue; and thence through said Elmwood avenue to the gate of Elmwood Cemetery. If the City of Detroit pave Croghan street, cotemporaneously with the laying of the track on said street, said Railway Company shall pave their track on said street, and two feet four inches on either side thereof, at their own expense. [*As amended by Ordinance approved March 3, 1865.*]

SEC. 3. The Railway through said streets shall be laid in the center thereof, if on a single track; and if on a double track, the inside rail of each track shall be laid a sufficient distance from the center of the street to enable two cars to pass on opposite tracks, and leave a space of at least eighteen inches; and the gauge of the track shall be at least four feet eight and one-half inches, and so as to accommodate the most common width of carriage wheels: *Provided, however,* That where a double track shall not be laid in the first instance, and a second track shall afterwards be required, such second track may be laid upon either side of the first: *And provided, further,* That in all streets which are not paved, or where plank roads are laid, the track of said Railway may be laid elsewhere than in the center thereof, as may be most convenient, under the direction of the Common Council, and shall least obstruct the public travel thereon. When the grantees shall complete one track of the said Railway, and place cars thereon for public use, they may, at any time thereafter, within five years, build a second track, so that they do not interrupt the running of their cars on the first completed track: *Provided,* The consent of the Common Council is first obtained.

SEC. 4. The track of said Railway shall be laid of such rails as are now laid in Woodward avenue, and as shall least obstruct the free passage of vehicles or carriages over the same; and the upper surface of the rails shall be laid flush with the surface of the streets, and shall conform to the grades thereof as now established, or as they shall, from time to time, be established or altered; and in case of grading, paving, or otherwise, if it be necessary to relay said rails, the same shall be done at the expense of the grantees; and in all streets, or parts of streets, which are not paved, the rails shall be laid in such manner as shall least interfere with the public travel thereon, and as shall be authorized and approved by the City Surveyor. The grantees and their assigns shall be required to keep the surface of the streets inside the rails, and for two feet four inches outside thereof, in good order and repair, and all snow, ice, dirt and filth cleared and removed from the same, in such a manner as will not obstruct the passage of said streets, at the expense of the grantees: *Provided, however*, That upon the paved portions of said streets, the materials for repaving shall be supplied at the expense of the City.

SEC. 5. The route of said Railway shall commence at that point on Fort street where said street intersects the westerly limits of the City of Detroit; from thence running to Elmwood avenue, on the course set forth in section two of this Ordinance; and in collecting fare, the whole of said distance shall be deemed but one route; and each passenger traveling the same continuously over the whole or any portion thereof, shall pay only one fare, the amount of which fare shall be five cents.

SEC. 6. Said railway shall be completed from the western limits of the City to Woodward avenue, on or before the first day of August, A. D. 1865, and the remainder thereof, from Woodward avenue to Elmwood avenue, on or before the twentieth day of August, A. D. 1866. [*As amended by Ordinance approved June 16, 1866.*]

SEC. 7. The cars to be used on said railways shall be drawn by animals only, at a speed not exceeding the rate of six miles per hour, and shall be run as often as public convenience shall require, and the Common Council shall prescribe: *Provided, always*, That said Council will not require them to run regular cars oftener than once in fifteen minutes, during sixteen hours every day, from the fifteenth day of April to the fifteenth day of October; and fourteen hours every day, from the fifteenth day of October to the fifteenth day of April, and the cars in use upon said railway shall be run for no other purpose that to transport passengers and their ordinary baggage; and the cars and carriages for that purpose shall be of the best style in use on said railways: *Provided*, that other cars and carriages may be used for constructing and repairing said railway tracks, and for cleaning the same from obstructions by snow or otherwise.

SEC. 8. The rate of fare for any distance shall not exceed five cents in any one car, on said route, except when cars or carriages shall be chartered for specific purposes: *Provided*, cars so chartered shall be so designated by placards, and shall not be considered regular cars within the meaning of the preceding section.

SEC. 9. Cars drawn in the same direction shall not approach within a distance of one hundred feet, except in cases of accident, or at stations, or for the purpose of connecting two cars together.

SEC. 10. No cars shall be allowed to stop on a cross-walk, or in front of any intersecting street, except to avoid collision or prevent danger to persons or property in the street.

SEC. 11. When the Conductor of any car is required to stop at the intersection of streets, to receive or leave passengers, the cars shall be stopped so as to leave the rear platform slightly over the crossing.

SEC. 12. The grantees or their assigns, shall employ careful, sober and prudent agents, conductors and drivers, to take charge of their cars while on the road; and it shall be the duty of all such agents, conductors and drivers, to keep vigilant watch for all trains, carriages or persons on foot, and especially for children, either upon the track, or moving towards it. At the first appearance of danger to such teams, carriages, footmen or children, or other obstructions, the cars shall be stopped in the shortest time and space possible, and the drivers shall be provided with a whistle for the purpose of sounding the alarm in case of danger.

SEC. 13. Conductors shall not allow ladies or children to enter or leave the cars while in motion.

SEC. 14. Conductors shall announce to the passengers the names of the principal squares and streets as the cars reach them.

SEC. 15. The cars shall at all times be entitled to the track, and any vehicles upon the track shall turn out when any car comes up, so as to leave the track unobstructed; and the driver of any vehicle refusing to do so, shall be liable to a fine not exceeding ten dollars, on conviction before the Recorder's Court of said City of Detroit; but costs and prosecution shall not be at the expense of the City: *Provided, however,* that the steam fire engines shall always have the right of the track on unpaved streets, when going to a fire.

SEC. 16. The cars after sunset, shall be provided with colored signal lights—a red light in front, and a green light in rear.

SEC. 17. Wherever gas or water pipes or sewers are now laid in the streets herein specified, and through which said railway is to pass, the said railway must be laid down and maintained, subject to the right now in the City, and the Gas Company and the Sewer and Water Commissioners to take up and remove said pipes or sewers in such a manner as not unnecessarily to damage or injure said railway or its use, without claim against said City, Gas Company or Water or Sewer Commissioners; and the Common Council expressly reserves to itself the right hereafter to lay down, or permit to be laid down, and repaired in said streets, gas or water pipes, and sewers, and pave said streets, whenever the Common Council shall so direct by resolution; the said gas or water companies, or private individuals, who shall take up pavement for the purpose aforesaid, being always required, as by the present City Ordinance, to restore the pavement in the streets to its former condition.

SEC. 18. If said grantees or their assigns shall fail to complete said railway, or any portion thereof, within the time prescribed by this Ordinance, then the rights and privileges herein granted, shall be forfeited as to the whole of said route herein established, and the City shall be entitled to take possession thereof, provided the Council does not extend the time: *Provided,* That if said grantees shall be delayed by the order or injunction of any Court, and said order or injunction shall not have been obtained at the instance or by the connivance of said grantees, then the time of such delay shall be excluded from the time of completion prescribed in this Ordinance.

Sec. 19. It is hereby reserved to the Common Council of the City of Detroit, the right to make such further rules, orders or regulations as may from time to time be deemed necessary to protect the interest, safety, welfare or accommodation of the public in relation to said railways.

Sec. 20. The powers and privileges conferred by the provisions of this Ordinance shall be limited to thirty years from and after the date of its passage.

Sec. 21. Said grantees shall, on or before the first day of March, A. D. 1865, deposit with the Controller of said City the sum of five thousand dollars in money or in United States Stocks, or in Treasury Notes bearing seven and three-tenths per cent interest, which deposit shall be security for the completion by said grantees of said line of railway, which they are required to construct and complete on or before the time herein mentioned for the completion of the same, and if the said railway shall not then be completed the sum so deposited shall be forfeited to the City.

Sec. 22. The said grantees and their assigns shall pay to the Treasurer of the City of Detroit, annually, twenty-five dollars on each and every passenger and other car, excepting only those cars used for constructing, repairing and cleaning the track on said road, to be collected as a license for the use of the City, after the term of five years from and after this date.

Sec. 23. Whenever said grantees, their successors or assigns, shall have organized themselves into a body politic and corporate, under the said act of the Legislature of the State of Michigan, and the amendment or amendments thereto, all the powers and privileges granted and conferred to and upon them by this Ordinance, shall be given, granted and duly vested in said corporation without any further action, consent, permission or authority of the Common Council whatever.

Sec. 24. No railway shall hereafter be built on and along the streets occupied by the railway herein provided for, for a greater distance than three blocks, at any one place, without the consent of the grantees and their successors.

Sec. 25. The rails of said street railway shall be laid on a foundation equal to that of Woodward avenue, or any other first-class railroad.

CHAPTER 50.

GRAND RIVER STREET COMPANY.

[Ordinance approved May 1, 1868.]

Whereas, Nathaniel Prouty, Moses F. Dickinson, William B. Wesson, Harvey King and James P. Mansfield, their associates, successors and assigns, propose to organize as a body politic and corporate under a charter from the Legislature of Michigan, or under the "Act to provide for the construction of tram railways," approved February 13, 1855 (Laws of 1855, p. 338), for the purpose of constructing and operating in and through the streets of the City of Detroit; therefore, be it ordained by the Common Council of the City of Detroit:

SECTION 1. That consent, permission and authority is hereby given, granted and duly vested in the said Nathaniel Prouty, Moses F. Dickinson, William B. Wesson, Harvey King, James P. Mansfield, their associates, successors and assigns, organized into a corporation under the laws of the State of Michigan as aforesaid, to lay a single or double track for a railway, with all the necessary and convenient tracks for turn-outs, side track and switches in and along the course of the streets and bridges in the City of Detroit hereinafter mentioned, and the same to keep, maintain and use and to operate thereon railway cars and carriages during all the term hereinafter specified and prescribed, and in the manner and upon the conditions set forth in the Ordinance: *Provided*, That nothing therein contained shall be construed to interfere with the legal rights of any of the plank roads running into the City of Detroit.

SEC. 2. The said grantees are hereby, by the provisions of this Ordinance, authorized to construct and operate railways, as herein provided, through Woodward avenue from Jefferson avenue; from said last named avenue to its intersection with Grand River street, and from thence on and through said Grand River street to the point of intersection with the railway tracks of the Michigan Southern & Detroit, Monroe & Toledo Railway tracks. And also on and through any other street or streets running between the western terminus above specified and Woodward avenue, from said Grand River street to the Detroit River, as the Common Council shall by resolution designate: *Provided,* That there shall not be at any time more than two parallel street railway tracks in Woodward avenue.

SEC. 3. All railways built, constructed, or maintained under the provisions of this Ordinance shall be laid in the center of any and each street wherein the same are built, constructed or maintained (save upon Woodward avenue), if on a single track; and if on a double track, the inside rail of each track shall be laid within two feet and four inches of the center of the street; the said rails shall be laid four feet and eight inches apart, so as to accommodate the most common width of carriage wheels: *Provided, nevertheless,* That in all streets which are not paved, or when plank roads are laid, the tracks of said railway may be laid elsewhere than in the center thereof, as may be most convenient, under the direction of the Common Council, and shall least obstruct the public travel thereon. When the grantees shall complete one track of the said railway, and place cars thereon, for public use, they may at any time thereafter, within five years, build a second track, so they do not interrupt the running of their cars on the first completed track: *Provided,* the consent of the Common Council is first obtained.

SEC. 4. The track of said Railway shall be laid of such rails as shall least obstruct the free passage of vehicles and carriages over the same; and the upper surface of the rails shall be laid flush with the surface of the streets, and shall conform to the grades thereof as now established, or as they shall, from time to time, be re-established or altered; and in case of grading, paving, or otherwise, if it be necessary to re-lay said rails, with necessary ties and stringers, the same shall be done at the expense of the grantees; and in all streets, and parts of streets, which are not paved, the rails shall be laid in such manner as shall least interfere with the public travel thereon, and as shall be authorized and approved by the City Surveyor. The grantees, or their assigns, shall be required to keep the surface of the streets inside of the rails in good order and repair, and all snow, ice, dirt and filth cleaned and removed from such portions of the streets at the expense of the grantees, and in such manner as not to obstruct travel in any part of the street.

Sec. 5. The cars to be used on said Railways shall be drawn by animals only, at a speed not exceeding the rate of six miles per hour, and shall be run as often as public convenience shall require, and the Common Council shall by resolution prescribe: *Provided, always,* That said Council will not require them to run regular cars oftener than once in twenty minutes during fourteen hours every day, from the fifteenth day of April to the fifteenth day of October, and twelve hours every day from the fifteenth day of October to the fifteenth day of April, and the cars and carriages used by said grantees shall be of the best style in use on street railways in this city, and the cars in use upou such railway shall be run for no other purpose than to transport passengers, and their ordinary baggage: *Provided,* That other cars and carriages may be used for cleaning said Railway tracks from obstructions by snow or otherwise.

Sec. 6. The rate of fare for any distance shall not exceed five cents in any one car, or on any one route named in this Ordinance, except where cars or carriages shall be chartered for specific purposes: *Provided,* Cars so chartered shall not be considered regular cars within the meaning of the preceding section.

Sec. 7. Cars drawn in the same direction shall not approach each other within a distance of one hundred feet, except in cases of accident or at stations, or for the purpose of connecting two cars together.

Sec. 8. The said grantees shall complete their Railway from Woodward avenue, through Grand River street, to the easterly line of the Woodbridge farm, cotemporaneously with the paving of said street to said easterly line of the Woodbridge farm; said Road thence from the easterly line of the Woodbridge farm to be completed to the western limits of the City as soon as the public necessity require it, and the Common Council shall be the judges of such necessity; and shall also complete their Road on any street designated by the Common Council, from Grand River street to the Detroit River, or to Jefferson avenue, within three months after such designation shall be made by said Council.

SEC. 9. No car shall be allowed to stop on a crosswalk, or in front of any intersecting street, except to avoid collision or prevent danger to persons or property in the street.

SEC. 10. When the conductor of any car is required to stop at the intersection of streets to receive or leave passengers, the cars shall be stopped so as to leave the rear platform slightly over the crossing.

SEC. 11. The grantees or their assigns shall employ careful, sober, and prudent agents, conductors, and drivers to take charge of their cars while on the Road, and it shall be the duty of all such agents, conductors, and drivers to keep vigilant watch for all trains, carriages, or persons on foot, and especially children, either upon the track, or moving towards it; at the first appearance of danger to such teams, carriages, footmen or childdren, or other obstructions, the cars shall be stopped in the shortest time and space possible.

SEC. 12. Conductors shall not allow ladies or children to enter or leave the cars while in motion.

SEC. 13. Conductors shall announce to the passengers the names of the principal squares and streets as the cars reach them.

SEC. 14. The cars shall at all times be entitled to the track, and any vehicles upon the track of said Railway shall turn out when any car comes up, so as to leave the track unobstructed, and the drivers of any vehicles refusing to do so, shall be liable to a fine not exceeding five dollars, on conviction before the Recorder's Court of said City of Detroit, and costs of prosecution shall not be at the expense of the City.

SEC. 15. The cars, after sunset, shall be provided with signal lights—blue in front, and green in rear of the cars.

Sec. 16. Wherever gas, or water pipes, and sewers, are now laid in the streets herein specified, and through which Railways are to pass, the said Railway must be laid down and maintained subject to the right now in the City, and the Gas Company, and Sewer and Water Commissioners to take up or remove said pipes or sewers in such a manner as not unnecessarily to damage or injure said Railways, or their use, without claim against said City, Gas Company, or Water or Sewer Commissioners; and the Common Council expressly reserves to itself the right hereafter to lay down, or to permit to be laid down, and repaired in said streets, gas, or water pipes, and sewers, whenever the public or private convenience may require; the said Gas or Water Companies, or private individuals, who shall take up pavement for the purposes aforesaid, being always required, as by the present City Ordinance, to restore the pavement in the street to its former condition.

Sec. 17. If said grantees or other assigns shall fail to complete any of the aforesaid railways within the time prescribed by this Ordinance, or by resolution of the Common Council, then the rights and privileges granted shall be forfeited as to any and every route herein established, which is not commenced and completed in the time herein prescribed, and the City shall be entitled to take possession thereof: *Provided*, The Council does not extend the time: *Provided*, That if said grantees shall be delayed by the order or injunction of any court: *Provided*, said injunction is not obtained by connivance of the said grantees: *And, provided further*, That if said grantees shall use due diligence to have said injunction removed, then the time of such delay shall be excluded from the time of completion prescribed in this Ordinance.

Sec. 18. It is hereby reserved to the Common Council of the City of Detroit, the right to make such further rules, orders or regulations, as may from time to time be deemed necessary to protect the interests, safety, welfare or accommodation of the public in relation to said railways.

Sec. 19. The powers and privileges conferred by the provisions of this Ordinance, shall be limited to thirty years from and after the date of its passage.

Sec. 20. This Ordinance shall be void and of no effect unless the grantees shall, within one month from the date of the passage thereof, notify the Common Council in writing of their acceptance of and agreement to the provisions of this Ordinance, and shall, within six months after said last date, commence the work of building and constructing said railway from Woodward avenue to the east line of the Woodbridge farm.

Sec. 21. It is distinctly provided, understood and agreed, that all the rights, franchises or privileges, hereby conferred upon the grantees, are subject to the rights now vested in the Detroit City Railway Company.

Sec. 22. If hereafter the said Grand River street shall be paved westerly of the easterly line of the Woodbridge farm, or any other street occupied by said Company, the said grantees shall, cotemporaneously with the paving of said street, at their own expense, pave all the portion of the street or streets which lies within their track, or any switches or turn-outs placed by them, such expenses to include the cost of grading, excavating, removal of earth, and all expenses necessary for paving the street to the extent above specified.

Sec. 23. The said grantees and their assigns shall pay to the Treasurer of the City of Detroit annually, after five years from the passage of this Ordinance, fifteen dollars on each and every passenger car, to be collected as a license for the use of the City after the term of five years from and after this date.

Sec. 24. Whenever the said grantees, their successors or assigns, shall have organized themselves into a body politic and corporate under the said act of the Legislature of the State of Michigan, all the powers and privileges granted and conferred to and upon them by this Ordinance shall be given, granted and duly vested in said corporation without any further action, consent, permission or authority of the Common Council whatever.

CHAPTER 51.

RAILROADS.

[Chapter thirty-nine of the Revised Ordinances of 1863.]

SECTION 1. The rate of speed of engines and cars on railroads, within the limits of the City, shall not exceed six miles per hour; and any engineer, driver, or conductor, having charge of an engine, car, or train of cars, upon any railroad in said City, who shall suffer or cause said engine, car, or train of cars, to go over said railroad, within said City, at a greater rate of speed than six miles an hour, shall be punished by a fine of not less than twenty-five dollars, nor more than one hundred dollars, or by imprisonment not to exceed six months, or by both said fine and imprisonment, in the discretion of the Court.

[Ordinance approved February 8, 1868.]

SEC. 2. All railroads, whose tracks are laid within the corporate limits of said City, shall place or cause to be placed, at every street crossing, and at a safe and proper distance, a suitable sign, lettered on both sides, to indicate a crossing, and to caution the public against any danger, immediate or remote, from an approaching locomotive or train of cars.

SEC. 3. Said sign shall be sixteen feet in height, and shall extend, when practicable, across the street where located; its particular construction or description and exact location to be under the direction of the Street Commissioner of the district where there may be any of said crossings.

SEC. 4. Whenever any railroad crossing, within the corporate limits of said City, shall be found without the sign, or signs, required by the Ordinance, it shall be the duty of the Street Commissioner of the district within which said crossing is situated, to serve a written notice on the Superintendent of the railroad, the track of which goes over the crossing, requiring him to cause said sign, or signs, to be erected within twenty days from the date of service of said notice, and if said Superintendent shall refuse, neglect, or fail to comply with said notice, the said Street Commissioner shall cause said sign, or signs, to be erected; and upon conviction of such neglect, or refusal, in the Recorder's Court, the Superintendent shall be fined in a sum not to exceed one hundred dollars and costs, in addition to the expense of erecting such sign, or signs; and in the imposition of any such fine and costs, the Court may make a further sentence, that in default of the payment thereof, said Superintendent shall be imprisoned in the Detroit House of Correction, or County Jail, for any period of time not exceeding six months.

[Ordinance approved February 8, 1868.]

SEC. 5. All railroad companies shall hereafter make up the trains for their roads within the grounds inclosed and occupied by them.

SEC. 6. Any violation of the provisions of this Ordinance shall be punished by a fine not to exceed one hundred dollars, and the offender may be imprisoned in the Detroit House of Correction until the payment thereof: *Provided, however,* That the term of such imprisonment shall not exceed ninety days.

[Ordinance approved September 30, 1869.]

SEC. 7. No person under the age of twenty-one years shall get on or off of any steam railway train, while in motion, within the limits of the City of Detroit, except at the respective depots of the Railroad Companies in said City.

SEC. 8. Any person violating the provisions of section one of this Ordinance shall be punished by a fine not exceeding ten dollars and costs; and in the imposition of any such fines and costs, the Court may make a further sentence, that in default of the payment thereof such offender be imprisoned in the Detroit House of Correction for any period of time not exceeding six months.

[Ordinance approved August 31, 1869.]

SEC. 9. That consent, permission and authority is hereby granted and duly vested in the Detroit Central Mills Company, their associates, successors and assigns, to lay and operate a single track Railway for the conveyance of freight by horse power in ordinary freight cars from the Detroit Central Mills across Woodbridge street, so as to connect with the Michigan Central Railroad track, as now laid: *Provided, however,* That said permission is granted subject to any compensation the owners of property along the route of said track may be entitled to; and *provided further,* That cars shall not be allowed to stand upon said street.

SEC. 10. Said track shall be laid at right angles with the carriage way on Woodbridge street, and the rails shall be of ordinary strap iron, laid flush with the surface of the pavement, in such manner as not to inconvenience the passage of vehicles; and the route of said track shall be in full accordance with the diagram filed in the office of the City Clerk, on the fifteenth day of June, 1869.

SEC. 11. It is hereby reserved to the Common Council of the City of Detroit the right to make further rules, orders or regulations as may, from time to time, be deemed necessary to protect the interest, safety, welfare or accommodation of the public in relation to said Railway, as well also the right to discontinue the use of said track at any time said Common Council deem it necessary to do so.

CHAPTER 52.

DEPARTURE AND ARRIVAL OF BOATS AND CARS.

[Chapter Fifty-eight of the Revised Ordinances of 1863.]

SECTION 1. No person shall, on the arrival of any railroad cars in said City, nor for the period of thirty minutes previously to the departure of any railroad cars from said City, have or keep any carriage, wagon, cart, or other vehicle, within twenty feet of the place where such railroad cars shall have ceased running, or are about to depart from said City.

SEC. 2. No person shall, on the arrival of any steamboat or vessel at any wharf in said City, nor for the period of thirty minutes thereafter, nor for the period of thirty minutes previous to the departure of such steamboats or vessels, have or keep any carriage, wagon, cart, or other vehicle, within sixty feet of the place where such steamboat or vessel has, or is about to be made fast, or depart from said City. Any person violating this, or the preceding section, shall, for every violation, on conviction before the Recorder's Court, forfeit a sum not exceeding one hundred dollars, and costs of prosecution.

SEC. 3. All carriages, wagons, carts, or other vehicles, the keepers whereof are waiting for employment from any railroad cars, steamboats or vessels, shall stand on either side of the street or alley, so as to leave the centre thereof, and access to each house thereon, open and unobstructed, for the free passage of carriages, wagons, carts, and other vehicles, and foot passengers. Any person violating this section, shall, for every violation, on conviction before the Recorder's Court, forfeit a sum not exceeding fifty dollars, and costs of prosecution.

SEC. 4. If any person shall, on the arrival or departure of any railroad cars, steamboats or vessels, at or from said City, or for the period of thirty minutes after the arrival, or before the departure of such railroad cars, steamboats or vessels, and within sixty feet of the wharf or depot where such railroad cars, steamboats or vessels have, or are about to stop running, or being made fast, or depart from said City, make, aid, countenance, or assist in making any loud or boisterous noise, disturbance, or improper diversion, or shall be guilty of any indecent, immoral or insulting conduct, language, or behavior, such person shall, for every such offense, on conviction before said Recorder's Court, forfeit a sum not exceeding one hundred dollars, and costs of prosecution.

SEC. 5. If any person shall, by any false, or deceitful representations to any stranger or traveler in said City, induce or prevail on such stranger or traveler to go to, and put up at any hotel, tavern, grocery, or other house of entertainment in said City, such person shall, for every such offense, on conviction before the Recorder's Court, forfeit a sum not exceeding one hundred dollars, and costs of prosecution.

SEC. 6. Nothing contained in the first and second sections of this Chapter shall be construed to prevent any teamster from hauling freight to any steamboat or vessel about to depart from said City.

SEC. 7. No propeller shall be permitted to approach within fifty feet of any wharf in this City, or lie at any wharf in this City, while fired up, unless her smoke pipe shall be covered with a good and sufficient spark catcher, or other covering, to prevent the emission of sparks or coals from her said pipe; and in case the captain or officers of any propeller shall permit the same to approach, or lie at any wharf, contrary to the provisions of this section, he or they shall be liable to a fine not exceeding one hundred dollars, to be recovered, with costs, by prosecution in the Recorder's Court.

CHAPTER 53.

STEAMBOATS AND VESSELS.

[Chapter Forty-two of the Revised Ordinances of 1866.]

SECTION 1. No steam tug or other vessel, while having one or more vessels in tow; and no vessel while made fast to any other vessel by lines or otherwise, shall approach within five hundred feet of any dock in said City, unless compelled to do so by unavoidable accident: *Provided*, This section shall not be so construed as to prevent steam tugs from approaching other vessels to take them in tow.

SEC. 2. No person shall throw or deposit in said river, within said limits, any substance which may, in any respect, tend to injure the navigation thereof.

SEC. 3. All steamboats, ships, brigs and other vessels shall have kept outboard during the night time a conspicuous light, elevated at least six feet above decks.

SEC. 4. All steamboats coming to or going from the docks, shall be moved under a low head of steam, and slowly, so as not to endanger the docks, or other crafts in port.

SEC. 5. No person shall unload any boat or vessel at or on any of the public wharves or docks in said City, or otherwise place or deposit on any such wharf or dock, any stone, lumber, timber, or firewood, or other material, without permission from the Harbor Master of said City.

SEC. 6. The Common Council may annually appoint, on the second Tuesday of January, or at any regular meeting of the Common Council thereafter, on the nomination of the Mayor of the City, a Harbor Master for the port of Detroit, who shall hold his office for one year, subject to removal under the Charter. His term of office to commence on the third Tuesday of January—the person appointed this summer to hold until the third Tuesday of January, 1863. Before entering upon his office he shall give bonds to the said City, with sufficient sureties, conditioned as required by the Revised Charter of the City.

SEC. 7. Such Harbor Master, when appointed as herein provided for, shall receive for his services one dollar and fifty cents a day, payable monthly: *Provided*, No salary shall be paid in any one year, for any such services, before the first day of April, and shall cease on the first day of December in each year.

SEC. 8. It shall be the duty of said Harbor Master to enforce the execution of the several provisions of this Ordinance, and of all other laws and ordinances passed in pursuance of the Revised Charter for regulating and preserving the navigation of said river within the limits of said City, and to make the necessary complaint for violations thereof.

SEC. 9. The Harbor Master authorized to be appointed by this Ordinance, shall have authority to protect the owners and occupants of wharves and docks within the limits of the City, in the free and undisturbed use of the same. And he is authorized to regulate the anchorage of all vessels lying within said City limits, and to give such orders and directions relative to the location and change of station of every steamboat, or other vessel, as shall be for the interests of trade and navigation, having respect at all times to the rights of occupants of wharves and docks; and to this end he shall have full authority to go on board of and move any steamboat or vessel that shall be, without right or consent, occupying any of said docks or wharves; and every owner, captain, master, consignee, or other person, having in charge any such steamboat or vessel, shall be liable to the penalties of this Ordinance for refusing to comply with such order or direction.

SEC. 10. Every owner, master, captain, consignee, or any other person having in charge any steamboats or other vessels used in violation of this Ordinance, and any person or persons violating or failing to comply with the provisions thereof, shall be punished by a fine not exceeding one hundred dollars and costs of prosecution; and in the imposition of any such fine and costs, the Court may make a further sentence that the offenders be imprisoned in the Detroit House of Correction until the payment thereof, for any term not exceeding six months.

SEC. 11. No owner, or agent, or person having the charge or control of any steamboat or other vessel, or any wreck of such steamboat or vessel, shall sink or deposit, or cause or suffer to be sunk or deposited, such boat, vessel or wreck, at any place or point in the Detroit River, lying within the limits of said City, and northeasterly of the northerly channel bank of said river, so as to obstruct or impair the navigation thereof; if any such owner, agent or person, having such charge and control of such boat, vessel or wreck, shall so sink, or deposit, or cause or suffer the same to be so sunk or deposited, or if the same be so sunk or deposited, within default, or intent, or design of any of the persons above mentioned, it shall be the duty of the Harbor Master to at once notify such owner, agent or person having control, to remove the same, and if the person or persons so notified refuse or neglect to remove the same within ten days after service of such notice the Harbor Master may cause the same to be removed, and the cost and expense of such removal shall be a claim and liability in favor of the City of Detroit against such person or persons; and such person or persons so refusing or neglecting shall be also subject to prosecution in the Recorder's Court for each day that such obstruction is allowed to continue after said ten days; and upon conviction shall be punished by a fine not exceeding five hundred dollars for each offense, and in the discretion of the Court may be sentenced to imprisonment in the House of Correction until the payment thereof: *Provided*, Such imprisonment shall not exceed the term of six months. [*Added by Ordinance approved March 7, 1868.*]

CHAPTER 54.

FERRIES.

[Chapter Forty-three of the Revised Ordinances of 1863.]

SECTION 1. No person shall keep a ferry or boat for carrying and transporting persons and property across the Detroit River to the opposite shore, without a license therefor from the Mayor.

SEC. 2. The Mayor is hereby authorized to grant a license as hereinafter provided, to any person, or company, to keep a ferry or boat to carry and transport persons and property across the Detroit River to the opposite shore, on his or their paying into the City Treasury the sum of fifty dollars for each boat which carries and transports passengers, teams and animals, and the sum of twenty-five dollars for each boat which transports and carries passengers only, and executing a bond to the City of Detroit in the penal sum of two hundred dollars, with one or more sureties, conditioned as provided in power sixty-three, of chapter five, of the City Charter.

SEC. 3. Any person or company desiring a license for a ferry to carry and transport persons across the Detroit River, shall make application therefor, in writing, to the Mayor; and such application shall state the points or wharves upon each shore between which it is proposed to run the ferry.

SEC. 4. The person or company licensed, as provided in section two, shall keep at all times, during the continuance of his or their license, a good and sufficient boat or boats, with a sufficient number of trusty and experienced hands to work and manage the same; and no ferry, while in use as such, between sunrise and seven o'clock P. M. of each day, shall be allowed to remain at their usual ferry landing for a longer period than five minutes between each trip, unless prevented from making trips across and back by the ice, or by said ferry being out of repair, and unable to ply as such ferry. [*As amended by Ordinance approved August 1, 1870.*]

SEC. 5. The granting of any license by the Mayor for a ferry between any wharves or points on each side of the Detroit River, shall not deprive him of the power to grant other licenses for ferries between the same points.

SEC. 6. No person or company licensed, as provided in this Ordinance, shall run his or their ferry between any other wharves or points than those designated in his or their application and license.

SEC. 7. No gaming, drunkenness, quarreling, fighting, blasphemy, or any rude, disorderly or immoral conduct, shall be allowed on any ferry.

SEC. 8. Persons and companies licensed to keep ferries, shall cause a list of the rates of ferriage to be printed in legible characters, and posted in a conspicuous place on their boat or boats.

SEC. 9. Ferriage, at any ferry established under this Ordinance, shall not exceed the following rates, to wit: For a foot passenger, except children under ten years of age, ten cents; and for such children, five cents. For a horse and rider, twenty cents. For a horse, fifteen cents. For one horse and vehicle, with two persons, twenty-five cents. For two horses and vehicle, with not more than four persons, fifty cents, and ten cents for each additional horse. For each head of horned cattle, ten cents. For each sheep or hog, five cents. For each one hundred pounds of baggage, or other article, five cents.

SEC. 10. The Mayor is hereby authorized to revoke any ferry license, whenever he shall be satisfied that the person or company keeping such ferry has intentionally violated any of the provisions of this Ordinance; and after such person or company, or its agent, has been notified of such revocation, it shall not be lawful to continue such ferry.

SEC. 11. Any violation of, or failure to comply with, the provisions of this Ordinance, shall be punished by a fine not to exceed two hundred dollars and costs; and in the imposition of any such fine and costs, the Court may make a further sentence, that in default of the payment thereof, such offender be imprisoned in the Detroit House of Correction or County Jail, for any period of time not exceeding six months.

TITLE V.

SEWERS.

CHAPTER 55.

PUBLIC AND PRIVATE DRAINS AND SEWERS.

[Chapter Forty-seven of the Revised Ordinances of 1863.]

SECTION 1. No person or persons shall be permitted to connect any drain from his, her, or their premises, with any public drain or sewer now made or constructed, or hereafter to be made or constructed, in said City, nor with any private drain, whereby his, her, or their premises will be drained into any public drain or sewer, except on previous application, in writing, to, and permission by the Common Council, or Board of Sewer Commissioners, and the payment of the assessment hereinafter mentioned.

SEC. 2. All private drains to be hereafter made by individuals in any public street, lane or alley, in said City, and connecting with any public drain or sewer, shall be of such size, dimensions and materials, and constructed and laid as directed by the Board of Sewer Commissioners, and shall enter such public drain or sewer under and according to the personal supervision and direction of their Engineer, nor shall any person or persons enter any public drain or sewer at any other places than those designated and fixed for that purpose in the construction thereof.

SEC. 3. The amount which individuals using or being benefited by any public drain or sewer, shall pay for such use, is hereby fixed as follows, to wit: the sum of one dollar and fifty cents annually, for each cellar drained directly or indirectly, into any public drain or sewer, which assessment shall be taken to include all other drainage of the premises to which said cellar especially belongs; and the sum of fifty cents annually for each lot, or subdivision of lot, being without a cellar, drained, as aforesaid, into any public drain or sewer; and such sums as may be fixed by the Common Council for all establishments requiring an unusual or extraordinary amount of drainage, drained as aforesaid, upon actual inspection of, and report thereon, by the Assessors. [*As amended by Ordinance approved January 2, 1866.*]

SEC. 4. Said assessment shall, in all instances, be paid when the City and School taxes are collected.

SEC. 5. Any person whose premises are drained, directly or indirectly, into any public drain or sewer, or any person using said premises thus drained, or for whose benefit or family the same is used, shall be liable to the payment therefor, and, in addition, said assessment shall become, and be a charge and lien on the premises thus drained, and be recovered, and the same proceedings had in every respect for the recovery thereof, as are provided for the recovery of other special assessments; and the Corporation may also, at their option, stop such private drain, and prevent any person from draining his premises into any public drain or sewer, where such assessment shall not be paid in advance, on the second application, and said privilege shall not be restored, unless on the payment of the tax, and a forfeiture of double the amount of the assessment.

SEC. 6. Any person who shall remove any grate from the pool over which it is placed, or in any way, directly or indirectly, injure any public drain or sewer, or any part thereof, shall, on conviction thereof, before the Recorder's Court, be liable to a penalty for each offense, not exceeding one hundred dollars, and costs.

SEC. 7. Any person who shall connect any drain from his premises with any public drain or sewer, or who shall drain his premises into any private drain which enters into any public drain or sewer, without first making the application, and procuring the permission provided for in the first section of this Chapter, shall, on conviction of each offense, before the Recorder's Court, be liable to a penalty, not exceeding one hundred dollars, and costs; and any person who shall construct and lay any private drain, connecting with any public drain or sewer, or who shall enter any public drain or sewer, in any other manner except as is provided for in the second section of this Chapter, shall be liable, for each offense, on like conviction, to a penalty not exceeding one hundred dollars, and costs; and any person who shall enter any public drain or sewer at any other place than is designated and fixed for that purpose in the construction thereof, shall be also liable to pay for each offense, on like conviction, a penalty not exceeding one hundred dollars, and costs; and if any person shall drain his premises along the side of any public drain or sewer, he shall also be liable to pay a penalty not exceeding one hundred dollars, and costs, on like conviction: *Provided*, That this section shall not be construed to extend to any case where a private drain has heretofore been laid down along the side of any public drain or sewer; but such private drain shall not be repaired by any person without having received from the Common Council, or Board of Sewer Commissioners, a certificate that such repair will not endanger the safety and preservation of any public drain or sewer along the side thereof. [*As amended by Ordinance approved January 2, 1866.*]

SEC. 8. No person shall be permitted to connect any drain from his premises with any public sewer without the consent of the Board of Sewer Commissioners; and any person offending against this section, shall, on conviction of such offense, before the Recorder's Court, be liable to pay a fine of one hundred dollars and costs. [*As amended by Ordinance approved January 2, 1866.*]

SEC. 9. All drains now made and constructed, or which shall hereafter be made and constructed by the Corporation, shall be deemed to be public drains or sewers, within the purview of this Chapter; and all sums of money received under the provisions of this Chapter, shall be stated and kept in a separate account, and are hereby specifically pledged and appropriated to the following uses and objects, and no other, to wit: *First*, To defray the expense of indispensable repairs of existing sewers; *Second*, To defray the cost of additional public sewers, and their repairs; *Third*, To apply on the interest of the City debt accruing on account of the cost of construction and maintenance of such sewers.

SEC. 10. The assessment provided for in this Chapter shall be collected in the manner prescribed by the Chapter relating to the collection of special assessments, the provisions of which are made applicable thereto, except that the time of the warrants, and provisions of per centage, shall be made to correspond with the terms of the warrants, and provisions for per centage, in the collection of the City and School taxes.

SEC. 11. No person shall be permitted to connect any drain from his, her, or their premises, with any drain or sewer made by one or more individuals, in any street, lane or alley, as aforesaid, unless on payment to the proprietors of such drain or sewer of a ratable proportion of the expense of making the same, the amount to be ascertained and determined by the City Surveyor, with the right of appeal to the Common Council; nor shall any person make or construct a sink, drain or sewer, leading into any other drain or sewer, without putting a sufficient strainer at the head of it, under a penalty not exceeding ten dollars, and costs, for each offense. [*As amended by Ordinance approved January 2, 1866.*]

SEC. 12. Every person having any drain from his, her, or their premises, that shall be connected with any drain or sewer now made, or that shall hereafter be made, as aforesaid, shall pay a ratable proportion of all expenses necessary for maintaining and keeping such drains or sewers in repair; such proportion to be ascertained and determined in the manner provided for in the foregoing section; and if any person shall neglect to pay the same, when so ascertained, such person shall forfeit and pay the sum of two dollars, and costs, for every week during which the same shall remain unpaid.

SEC. 13. In all cases where drains or sewers shall be obstructed so as to become, in the opinion of the Board of Sewer Commissioners, a nuisance, it shall be their duty to give notice to the persons using the same, to repair such drains or sewers, and if the same be not forthwith repaired, it shall be their duty to cause the necessary repairs to be made, and to charge the said persons with a ratable proportion of the expense incurred, subject to an appeal to the Common Council, as is provided in the tenth section; and all such appeals shall be made within the time in which such person is required to pay the sums above required; and if any person shall refuse or neglect to pay their proportion of the charges, for the space of ten days after notice, he or they shall be liable, upon conviction, before the Recorder's Court, to pay a fine not exceeding fifty dollars, and costs of suit. [*As amended by Ordinance approved January 2, 1866.*]

SEC. 14. No connection with public or private sewers, or drains, shall be made under the provisions of this Chapter, until the Surveyor shall have designated the grade therefor, under the penalty of twenty dollars.

SEC. 15. Any person or persons owning a lot or lots in the vicinity of a public sewer, will henceforth be required to drain such lot or lots into a sewer lying adjacent thereto, whenever the Committee on Health decide upon the necessity for so doing; and the drain from such lot or lots must be constructed under the supervision of the Sewer Commissioners. [*Added by Ordinance approved September 22, 1865.*]

SEC. 16. If any person or persons owning or occupying such lot or lots shall neglect or refuse to comply with the requirements of the foregoing section, within ten days after a written notice has been served upon him or them by a member of the Metropolitan Police, under authority or instructions from the Committee on Health; or, if such lot or lots be vacant, and no owner or agent of same can be found within the City, after a written notice has been posted up on the lot or lots for the period aforesaid, by a member of said police, then the person whose premises are thus drained, or any person using said premises thus drained, or for whose benefit or family the same is used, shall be liable to the payment therefor; and in addition, said assessment shall become and be a charge and lien on the premises thus drained, and be recovered; and the same proceedings had in every respect for the recovery thereof as are provided for the recovery of other special assessments. [*Added by Ordinance approved September 22, 1865.*]

[Ordinance Approved June 1, 1866.]

SEC. 17. Whenever the Common Council or the Board of Health shall deem it necessary that any occupied lot or lots in said City should be drained, they shall cause a notice, written or printed, or partly written and partly printed, to be served by some member of the Metropolitan Police, upon the owner, agent or occupant of such lot or lots, to construct a private drain or sewer therefrom, connecting with some public drain or sewer, to be designated in the notice; such notice shall be served personally upon the persons to be notified, if they are found, and, if not found, by posting the same in some public place upon the premises.

SEC. 18. Whenever, in the opinion of the Board of Health, any lot, or lots, or premises, whether occupied or not, shall, for want of sufficient drainage, become dangerous to the public health, or a nuisance, such Board shall cause a notice, written or printed, or partly written and partly printed, to be served by a member of the Metropolitan Police upon the owner, agent or occupant of such lot or lots, or premises, to construct a private drain or sewer therefrom to connect with some public drain or sewer, to be designated in the notice. Such notice shall be served personally upon the parties to be notified, if found, and, if not found, by posting the same in some conspicuous place on the premises.

SEC. 19. If the person or persons so notified shall neglect or refuse, for ten days after the service of this notice, to comply with the requirements thereof, it shall be the duty of the Board of Sewer Commissioners to at once cause the required drain or drains, sewer or sewers, to be constructed so as to well and sufficiently drain such premises. The Board of Sewer Commissioners shall also, upon the completion of the work, file at the office of the Receiver of Taxes, a statement showing the work done, the entire cost thereof, and apportioning such cost in just proportions upon the several lots or premises drained. Such apportionment shall be final and binding upon all parties. From the time of filing such statement the amount of cost so proportioned shall be a lien upon the lot, or lots, or premises, respectively, to the extent so apportioned to them, and the same proceedings shall be had in every respect for the enforcement and collection thereof as are provided for the enforcement and collection of special assessments. The person or persons so neglecting or refusing to comply with the requirements of any notice served under any of the foregoing provisions, shall, in case there is a drain or sewer with which the proposed drain or sewer may connect, within fifty feet of the lot, lots or premises specified in the notice, also be liable to prosecution in the Recorder's Court, and, upon conviction of such neglect or refusal, shall be punished by a fine not exceeding twenty-five dollars and costs. And the offender may also be sentenced to imprisonment in the Detroit House of Correction for a period not exceeding six months, or until such fine and costs are paid.

SEC. 20. All private drains or sewers, constructed under the provisions of this Ordinance, shall be constructed under the supervision of the Board of Sewer Commissioners.

CHAPTER 56.

LATERAL SEWERS.

[Ordinance approved April 2, 1870.]

SECTION 1. The Common Council may, by resolution, direct the construction, cleansing, or repair of lateral sewers or drains, through, or in any streets or alleys, or the construction, cleansing, or repairs of drains from any house, yard, or lot, when, in their opinion, the same shall be necessary. Such drains or sewers to be built of such materials as the Board of Sewer Commissioners shall direct, and be laid or constructed in such direction, of such size and width, such descent, and with such strainers or grates, as said Sewer Commissioners shall direct: *Provided*, That no wooden box or drain shall be constructed or laid in any public street, lane or alley in said City, but that all sewers or drains constructed or laid in said streets, lanes, or alleys, shall be of brick, or crocks, or such other material as the Sewer Commissioners shall approve.

SEC. 2. Whenever the Common Council shall direct, as aforesaid, the construction, cleansing, or repair of any lateral sewer or drain, as provided for in section one, it shall be the duty of the City Surveyor to assess the expense of constructing, cleansing, or repairing the same, in a ratable proportion, to the owners or occupants of all land or lots adjoining said street or alley, or to the owner or occupant of the land or lot through which such drain shall run; and it shall be the duty of the Sewer Commissioners, whenever such resolution shall be passed, to cause notice of the intended improvement to be served on the owners of all lots or premises intended to be assessed; such notice shall be served personally on such owner, or his agent, or by leaving the same at the residence of such owner or agent, or in case they or their residence cannot be found, the same shall be served on any occupant of the premises, and if the same be unoccupied, by posting the same in some conspicuous place upon the premises. The said Sewer Commissioners shall file with the City Clerk a due certificate of their doings, and all persons served with notice in either of the modes herein provided, who do not make and file objections before its confirmation by the Common Council, shall be precluded from thereafter questioning or making any objections to the assessment roll for such improvement, and the following form of notice shall be sufficient:

"No. SEWER COMMISSIONERS' OFFICE,
DETROIT, 18 .

"To

"You are hereby notified that the Common Council has ordered an assessment to be made for the construction of a lateral sewer in

And that all persons interested in any lands or lots adjoining said streets or alleys, claiming to have the same exempted for building said lateral sewer, are requested to show the reasons therefor to the Common Council, at its next regular session, after the expiration of five days from the date of this notice.

"President of Sewer Commissioners."

"STATE OF MICHIGAN,
COUNTY OF WAYNE, } ss.
City of Detroit.

"I hereby certify that I served the foregoing notice, as follows:"

SEC. 3. On confirmation of the assessment rolls by the Common Council, the City Clerk shall deposit said rolls with the City Controller, and said Controller shall thereupon place said rolls in the hands of the Receiver of Taxes, and, upon the receipt of said rolls by the Receiver of Taxes, he shall advertise a notice that said rolls are in his office, and the amounts assessed are due, and payable at said office for thirty days; at the expiration of which time the Controller shall issue a warrant to the City Collector of said City, with a command to levy and collect all sums and assessments then remaining unpaid, with the cost and charges thereon, and five cents on the dollar for his services, by distress and sale of the goods and chattels of the person against whom said assessment has been made, or those who may be liable to pay the same; and, further, commanding the City Collector to make returns to the Common Council within five days thereafter.

SEC. 4. Upon receiving the assessment roll, or a copy thereof, and warrant, it shall be the duty of the City Collector to proceed to demand and collect the several sums mentioned therein, and if any person shall neglect or refuse to pay the same, then, if he can find any goods or chattels of the person liable therefor, he shall levy thereon, and shali proceed to sell such goods and chattels at public auction, to the highest bidder, and shall render the surplus (if any), after deducting costs and charges, of such distress and sale, to the person entitled thereto.

SEC. 5. No parties, except those embraced in the said assessment roll, shall connect with any such lateral sewer or drain, without permission of the Sewer Commissioners, and without payment to the Receiver of Taxes of such sum or sums as the City Surveyor shall decide it to be right and proper for them to pay; and any person or persons who shall violate this Section shall be prosecuted before the Recorder's Court, and fined not to exceed one hundred dollars, and costs of prosecution, and the amount so decided upon by the Surveyor shall also be recovered before said Court.

SEC. 6. Whenever an assessment shall be ordered to be made under this Ordinance, it shall be the duty of the City Clerk of the said City to publish a notice for five days in the daily newspaper published by the contractor to do the printing of the City, which said notice shall state the fact that said assessment has been ordered by the Common Council, the purposes for which it has been ordered, and that said Common Council will, at their next regular meeting, after the expiration of said five days, permit any person whose lot or premises are liable to be included in said assessment, to show to said Council why said lot or premises should not be assessed.

CHAPTER 57.

SEWER POOLS.

[Chapter Forty-nine of the Revised Ordinances of 1863.]

SECTION 1. It shall be and hereby is made the duty of Overseers of Highways to clean and keep open and unobstructed the grates or other openings of pools within their respective Wards, connecting with any of the public sewers of said City, so that, at all times, said grates or other openings shall be unobstructed, and in condition to perform the office of carrying off the water from the public streets of said City.

CHAPTER 58.

ASSESSMENT FOR DRAINAGE.

[Chapter Fifty-two of the Revised Ordinances of 1863.]

SECTION 1. It is made the duty of the City Assessor, once in each year, to ascertain and place upon the assessment rolls all lots, premises or subdivisions thereof drained by private sewers, or drains leading into or connected with any public sewer or drain; and he shall designate on said rolls every lot, premises or subdivisions thereof, on which there is a cellar; and every lot, premises or subdivisions thereof, drained as aforesaid, on which there is no cellar; and also every lot, premises or subdivision thereof on which there is any hotel, tavern, tannery, or any kind of manufactory.

TITLE VI.

MARKETS AND SALES.

CHAPTER 59.

STALLS AND STANDS IN PUBLIC MARKETS.

[Chapter Fifty-three of the Revised Ordinances of 1863.]

SECTION 1. The square of ground lying between the east end of the City Hall and the west line of Randolph street, is hereby declared to be a Public Market, and shall constitute and be known as the City Hall Market.

SEC. 2. The Common Council may, from time to time, establish, in addition to the City Hall Market, such other Public Markets as the convenience and necessities of the City may require.

SEC. 3. The City Controller and the Committee on Markets shall, in the month of March in each year, establish and grade the minimum rent to be paid per month upon all the meat stalls and vegetable and fish stands in the Public Markets, and when so established as aforesaid, the same shall be reported to the Common Council by the Controller for confirmation. Thereupon that body shall immediately take action upon said matter, and it shall be the duty of the Controller and Committee on Markets, on or before the first day of April in each year, to lease to responsible and proper persons all stalls and stands, which may be applied for if not then already leased, the stalls in the meat markets to be leased for the term of one year, and the stands in the vegetable markets for the term of seven months; but no stall or stand shall be leased at a rent below the minimum established by the Common Council. Any stall or stand which shall not be so rented on or before the first day of April, may, at any time, be rented by the Controller to any responsible person for any period not extending beyond the first day of April of the following year, at a rent not less than the minimum established by the Common Council, and no person shall be allowed to rent more than two stalls in the meat markets. [*As amended by Ordinance approved November 3, 1870.*]

SEC. 4. All persons leasing or renting stalls or stands in the Public Markets of the City, shall pay the same monthly in advance; and each lessee of a stall in the meat market shall, with one or more sureties, to be approved by the Controller, enter into a lease with the City of Detroit, conditioned for the payment of the rent of such stall, in the manner herein provided, and for the faithful observance of the provisions of all Ordinances relative to the Public Markets of the City.

SEC. 5. The Controller shall make out and deliver to the Clerk of the Market a monthly roll of the amounts due for rents to the City from persons occupying stalls and stands in the Public Markets, and it shall be the duty of the Clerk to collect the same.

SEC. 6. If the lessee of any stall or stand shall neglect, for five days after notice that the same has become due, to pay the rent thereof, such lease shall be thereby forfeited, and it shall be the duty of the Controller to enter and take possession of such stall or stand on behalf of the City; and the City Attorney or other proper officer of the City, shall at once commence legal proceedings to collect such rent.

SEC. 7. If any lessee of any stall or stand whose lease shall have been forfeited, or any other person without a lease from the City, shall hold, use or occupy any stall or stand in a Public Market, he shall forfeit and pay to the City of Detroit, ten dollars for each day he shall so hold, use, or occupy any such stand.

SEC. 8. No lessee of any stall or stand shall permit the same to to be used or occupied by any other person, except by permission of the Controller or Committee on Markets: *Provided*, That not more than one person occupy one stall at the same time.

SEC. 9. The Public Markets of the City shall be kept open every day, Sunday excepted, for such hours as may be, from time to time, fixed by the Controller and Committee on Markets.

SEC. 10. The Committee on Markets and City Controller shall have power, and it shall be their duty, from time to time, to make rules and regulations for the government of the Public Markets of the City, which shall be submitted to the Common Council for its approval; and such rules and regulations, when approved, shall be printed and distributed among the persons leasing and occupying stalls and stands in the Public Markets. [*As amended by Ordinance approved November 3, 1870.*]

SEC. 11. The Committee on Markets and the Controller, shall from time to time, determine and submit to the Council, for approval, the amount per day to be paid for each wagon, cart, and other vehicle standing in the market, and from which vegetables, fish, poultry, eggs, butter or fruits are sold, and shall also establish and determine the places to be occupied by such wagons, carts or other vehicles. [*As amended by Ordinance approved November 3, 1870.*

CHAPTER 60.

CASS MARKET.

[Ordinance approved August 17, 1866.]

SECTION 1. That certain lot or parcel of land, situate and being in the Fifth Ward of said City, bounded by Adams avenue, Cass avenue and Grand River road, and being the same conveyed to the City of Detroit, by Lewis Cass, by deed, bearing date the twenty-second day of August, A. D. 1865, and recorded in the Register's office for the county of Wayne, in Liber one hundred and eight, at page five hundred and ninety-four, *et. seq.*, is hereby declared to be a Public Market, and shall constitute and be known as Cass Market.

SEC. 2. The said market and all stalls and places therein, shall be governed, controlled and leased in conformity with, and in pursuance of the Ordinances and rules in force for the time being, in reference to the Public Markets in said City, which rules and

Ordinances are hereby made applicable to the market hereby established. [*As amended by Ordinance approved November 3, 1870.*

CHAPTER 61.

PUBLIC MARKETS.

[Chapter fifty-four of the Revised Ordinances of 1863.]

SECTION 1. All persons selling, or offering for sale, from wagons, carts or other vehicles, any vegetables, fish, poultry, butter or fruits in the vicinity of the City Hall Market, shall occupy and stand with their teams on that portion of Michigan avenue embraced between the east line of the City Hall, and the east line of Randolph street.

SEC. 2. No butcher, forestaller, grocer, trader, or other person, shall sell or offer for sale, at any place within the limits of the City of Detroit, any unsound, nauseous or unwholesome meat, poultry, fish, vegetables, fruits or other articles of food or provisions, or the flesh of any animal dying otherwise than by slaughter, or poultry from which the entrails, crop and head have not been removed; nor any impure or spurious wines or spirituous liquors; nor any unwholesome bread, cake or pastry, manufactured in whole or in part from unwholesome flour or meal. [*As amended by Ordinance approved March 6, 1866.*

SEC. 3. No person, within any of the Public Markets of this City, shall be guilty of any lewd, lascivious or disorderly conduct, or make any loud or boisterous noises, or use any profane or vulgar language, or do any act which is calculated to lead to a breach of the peace, or which tends to disturb the good order and decorum of the place.

SEC. 4. No person shall resist or obstruct the Clerk of the Market in the execution of his duties.

SEC. 5. All meat, poultry and provisions of every kind, sold in the Public Markets, shall be weighed or measured by scales, weights, or patent balances, or in measures duly tested and stamped by the City Inspector of Weights and Measures.

SEC. 6. No person shall kill or slaughter within the limits of any Public Market any beast, or gut or cleanse any fish, or lay or throw or deposit any dirt, filth, dung, garbage or offal therein.

SEC. 7. No person whose stock in trade shall exceed the sum of three hundred dollars, shall be allowed to sell or offer for sale in the Public Markets of the City, any merchandise or clothing of any description whatever, or any glass, china or earthenware, books and stationery.

SEC. 8. No person shall sell at auction any goods, wares or merchandise, or furniture of any kind, within the limits of any Public Market, during market hours.

SEC. 9. No person shall slaughter or expose for sale the meat of any calf less than three weeks old.

SEC. 10. No person shall burn, sear or cut the inner part of the mouth of any calf, or confine the mouth of any calf by rope, twine or any kind of muzzle placed over the mouth of such calf. And no person shall in any manner tie or confine by rope, twine or otherwise, the feet of any calf, sheep, lamb or swine, or poultry, which may be brought to the City for sale. [*As amended by Ordinance approved June 1, 1865.*]

SEC. 11. Any violation of the provisions of this Ordinance shall be punished by a fine not to exceed one hundred dollars, and costs of prosecution, and the offender may be sentenced to be confined in the Detroit House of Correction till the payment thereof: *Provided,* Such imprisonment shall not exceed the period of six months.

CHAPTER 62.

THE SALE OF CALVES, SHEEP, AND LAMBS IN WAGONS.

[Chapter Fifty-six of the Revised Ordinances of 1863.]

SECTION 1. Persons owning, or having in charge, any vehicle loaded with, or containing live calves, sheep or lambs, shall not permit the same to stand in any street, avenue, alley or public space in the City of Detroit, except in one of the Public Markets, at such place or places as the Clerk of the Market shall direct; and such persons shall stricly comply with the rules and regulations prescribed for the good order and governent of the markets.

SEC. 2. The Clerk of the Market shall be entitled to demand and receive from the owner or person having in charge any such vehicle, as referred to in section one, and such persons shall pay, before offering any such calves, sheep or lambs for sale, the sum of ten cents for each calf, and five cents for each sheep or lamb; which shall be paid over by the Clerk as other moneys secured by him.

SEC. 3. Any violation of, or failure to comply with the provisions of this Ordinance, shall be punished by a fine not exceeding one hundred dollars and costs; and in the imposition of any such fine and costs, the Court may make a further sentence that the offender shall be committed to the Detroit House of Correction or to the County Jail, until the same be paid, for any period of time not exceeding six months.

CHAPTER 63.

PLATFORM SCALES.

[Ordinance Approved November 3, 1870.]

SECTION 1. The business of weighing produce, meat by the quarter, provisions, and such other articles as are brought to the City Hall Market, by wagon or other conveyance, for sale, shall be done by persons who shall be designated by the Committee on Markets and Controller, and approved by the Common Council, and each of whom shall be licensed at twenty-five dollars per annum, payable in advance. They shall enter into a bond in the sum of one hundred dollars each, with one or more good and sufficient sureties, for the faithful performance of their duties, and the strict observance of the rules and Ordinances governing the market; they shall provide themselves at their own expense, with a good portable platform scale; they shall receive such fees for weighing as may be fixed by said Common Council. They shall be subject to the rules, regulations and penalties applicable to persons renting stalls and stands in said Market, and all other rules governing said Market now in force, or which may hereafter be adopted and published.

CHAPTER 64.

PRIVATE MEAT MARKETS.

[Chapter fifty-five of the Revised Ordinances of 1863.]

SECTION 1. No person shall keep or continue any stall, booth, or stand in the City of Detroit, for the sale of fresh meat, without a license from the Mayor, as provided in the next section.

SEC. 2. The Mayor is hereby authorized to grant a license to any resident of the City of Detroit to keep a stall, booth or stand in the City of Detroit, for the purpose of selling fresh meat, on such person paying into the City Treasury the sum of five dollars, and and executing a bond to the City of Detroit in the penal sum of two hundred dollars, with one or more sureties, conditioned that he will faithfully observe the provisions of this Ordinance.

SEC. 3. It shall be the duty of any person licensed under this Ordinance, to keep his stall, booth or stand in a clean and orderly condition.

SEC. 4. No person licensed under this Ordinance shall sell, or expose for sale, any unwholesome, emaciated, blown, stuffed, tainted, bruised, putrid, unsound, or measly meat, poultry or provisions.

SEC. 5. Any person violating the provisions of this Ordinance shall be punished by a fine not to exceed one hundred dollars, and costs of prosecution; and the Court may sentence the offender to be imprisoned in the Detroit House of Correction until such fine and costs be paid: *Provided, however,* That the term of such imprisonment shall not exceed the period of six months.

CHAPTER 65.

THE PEDDLING OF MEAT.

[Chapter Sixty-one of the Revised Ordinances of 1863.]

SECTION 1. No person shall peddle, sell, or offer for sale, from any wagon, cart or vehicle, in or about the Public Markets, or in any street of the City of Detroit, any beef, pork, mutton or other meats, except venison, by the carcass or quarter, without a license from the Mayor, as hereinafter provided. This section shall not be construed to require any farmer, who shall sell or offer for sale any meat which shall have been fatted and killed by him, to take out a license, as provided in the next section.

SEC. 2. The Mayor is hereby authorized to license any person to follow the business of a peddler or hawker of meat, on such person paying into the treasury the sum of twenty-five dollars, and executing a bond to the City of Detroit, with one or more sureties, in the penal sum of one hundred dollars, and conditioned that such person shall faithfully observe the provisions of the Charter and Ordinances of the Corporation.

SEC. 3. Any violation of the provisions of this Ordinance shall be punished by a fine not to exceed one hundred dollars, and costs of prosecution; and the offender may be sentenced to be imprisoned in the Detroit House of Correction until the payment thereof: *Provided, however*, That the term of such imprisonment shall not exceed the period of six months.

CHAPTER 66.

MANUFACTURE AND SALE OF BREAD.

[Ordinance Approved April 21, 1870.]

SECTION 1. It shall not be lawful for any person to use or carry on the trade or business of a baker, either in person or by employing any other person to use or carry on the said trade or business, under his or her direction, or for his or her profit or benefit, within said City, without having obtained from the Common Council a permit for that purpose.

SEC. 2. Every person desirous to use or carry on said trade or business, shall make application in writing to the Common Council, setting forth the street and the number of the place of business in which he or she intends to carry on said trade or business; and if the Common Council shall grant such application, the City Clerk shall deliver such person a permit for the purpose aforesaid, for which he shall be entitled to receive from such person the sum of twenty-five cents; and the said permit shall be in force till the second Tuesday in March then next ensuing.

SEC. 3. The said Clerk shall record in a book, to be kept in his office for public inspection, the name, street and number of place of business of each person to whom he shall issue a permit, as provided in section two of this Ordinance.

SEC. 4. All bread of every description manufactured by the bakers of this City for sale, shall be made of good and wholesome flour or meal into loaves of one pound, two pounds, and four pounds, and no other, avoirdupois weight; and no baker shall make for sale, or shall sell or expose for sale any bread that shall be deficient in weight, according to the requisitions prescribed in the preceding section of this Chapter: *Provided, always,* That such deficiency in the weight of such bread shall be ascertained by the Sealer of Weights and Measures, by weighing or causing to be weighed in his presence, within eight hours after the same shall have been baked, sold or exposed for sale: *And provided, further,* That whenever any allowance in the weight shall be claimed on account of any bread having been baked, sold or exposed for sale more than eight hours as aforesaid, the burden of proof in respect to the time when the same shall have been baked, sold or exposed for sale, shall devolve upon the defendant or baker of such bread.

SEC. 5. The Sealer of Weights and Measures, under the direction of the Chief of Police, shall be Inspector of Bread, and it shall be his duty, and he is hereby authorized and required from time to time and not less than once in each month, at all seasonable hours, to enter into, and inspect and examine every baker's shop, storehouse or other building where any bread is or shall be baked, stored or deposited, or offered for sale, and to inspect and examine all bread found therein, and also to stop, detain and examine, in any part of said City, any person or persons, wagons or other carriages, carrying any loaf of bread for the purpose of sale, and weigh the same, and determine whether the same are in violation of the true intent and meaning of this Chapter; and if the said Inspector shall find any bread not conformable to the directions herein contained, or any part of them, he shall make complaint thereof for the purpose of having such person prosecuted according to law.

SEC. 6. No person or persons shall obstruct, or in any manner impede or willfully delay the said Sealer of Weights and Measures in the execution of his duties under this Ordinance, either by refusing him or delaying his entrance or admission into any of the places above mentioned, or refuse or omit to stop their wagon or carriage as aforesaid, whereby the due execution of this Ordinance or any part of it shall be impeded or obstructed.

SEC. 7. Any violation of any of the provisions of this Ordinance shall be punished by a fine not to exceed fifty dollars, and the costs of prosecution, and the offender may be imprisoned in the Detroit House of Correction until the payment thereof: *Provided, always,* That the term of such imprisonment shall not exceed the period of six months.

CHAPTER 67.

HAWKERS AND PEDDLERS.

[Chapter Sixty-three of the Revised Ordinances of 1863.]

SECTION. 1. No person shall follow the business or occupation of a hawker or peddler, within the limits of the City of Detroit, without a license from the Mayor.

SEC. 2. The Mayor is hereby authorized to license any person to follow the business or occupation of a hawker or peddler, on his paying into the City Treasury the sum prescribed in the next section, and executing a bond to the City of Detroit in the penal sum of one hundred dollars, with one or more sureties, conditioned that the person licensed will faithfully observe the provisions of the Charter and Ordinances of the Corporation.

SEC. 3. Any person soliciting a license, shall pay therefor as follows: If he intends to travel on foot, the sum of five dollars; if he intends to travel with one horse, or other animal, the sum of ten dollars; and if he intends to travel with two or more horses, or other animals, the sum of fifteen dollars.

SEC. 4. This Ordinance is not intended to apply to any mechanic of this State, selling, or offering for sale, any article of his own manufacture or construction, nor to any person selling, or offering for sale, any vegetables, berries, fruit, butter or eggs.

SEC. 5. Any person violating any of the provisions of this Ordinance, shall be punished by a fine not to exceed fifty dollars and costs; and in the imposition of any fine and costs, the Court may make a further sentence, that in default of the payment of such fine and costs, the offender be imprisoned in the Detroit House of Correction, or County Jail, for any period of time not exceeding six months.

CHAPTER 68.

AUCTIONEERS.

[Chapter Sixty-four of the Revised Ordinances of 1863.]

SECTION. 1. No person shall exercise the business or trade of an Auctioneer, or sell property by public auction or outcry, without a license from the Mayor. This section shall not apply to any person selling property by virtue of a legal process, or under a mortgage.

SEC. 2. The Mayor is authorized to grant a license to any resident of Detroit, of good character, or to any non-resident or transient person of good character, on the conditions prescribed in the following section.

SEC. 3. Any resident, applying for a license, shall, before the issuing thereof, pay into the City Treasury, the sum of ten dollars, and execute a bond to the Corporation, in the sum of five hundred dollars, with two sufficient sureties, conditioned for a faithful observance of the Charter and Ordinances of the City. If he be a non-resident, he shall, before the issuing of the license, pay the sum of ten dollars for each and every day he proposes to sell, and execute a similar bond, as hereinbefore prescribed for residents.

SEC. 4. In addition to the sum above mentioned to be paid

for license, each auctioner shall pay the sum of one per cent upon the amount of all moneys received, or to be received from the sale of goods brought from without the City, sold by auction. [*As amended by Ordinance approved July 27, 1870.*]

SEC. 5. No bell or crier shall be used to collect bidders at any auction.

SEC. 6. It shall be lawful for any auctioneer to sell on any wharf, or in any street, the following articles, to wit: Molasses, oils, wines, or any other liquors or liquids, the sale of which is authorized by law, contained in half barrels, barrels, casks, hogsheads, or other vessels, ship furniture and tackle, carriages, farming utensils, household furniture, and goods or merchandise, in packages or parcels, which shall weigh one hundred pounds: *Provided, however,* That such auctioneer shall not obstruct or encumber any wharf or street, so as to interfere with travel.

SEC. 7. Any violation of the provisions of this Ordinance shall be punished by a fine not to exceed one hundred dollars and costs; and in the imposition of any fine and costs, the Court may make a further sentence, that in default of the payment thereof, within a time to be fixed in such sentence, the offender be imprisoned in the Detroit House of Correction, or County Jail, for any period of time not exceeding six months.

CHAPTER 69.

PAWNBROKERS.

[Chapter Sixty-five of the Revised Ordinances of 1863.]

SECTION 1. No person shall engage in the business of a pawnbroker, in the City of Detroit, without a license from the Mayor, as hereinafter provided.

SEC. 2. The Mayor is hereby authorized to grant a license to any person of good character, to engage in the business of a Pawnbroker in the City of Detroit, on his paying into the City Treasury, the sum of fifty dollars, and executing a bond to the City of Detroit, in the penal sum of one thousand dollars, with one or more sufficient sureties, to be approved by the Mayor, conditioned that he will faithfully observe the provisions of the Charter and Ordinances of the City, as provided in subdivision sixty-three, of Chapter five, of the Charter of the City of Detroit.

SEC. 3. No person licensed as a Pawnbroker, under this Ordinance, shall, by virtue of one license, keep more than one house, shop or place for taking goods in pawn.

SEC. 4. Every person licensed under this Ordinance, shall cause his name, or the name of the firm, with the words "Licensed Pawnbroker," to be printed in large legible characters, and placed over the outside of the door of his shop, or place of business.

SEC. 5. Every pawnbroker shall keep a book, in which shall be legibly written, at the time of each loan, an accurate description of the goods, article or thing pawned, the time of pledging the same, the amount of money loaned thereon, the rate of interest to be paid on such loan, the time within which such pawn is to be redeemed, and the name and residence of the person pledging the said goods, article or thing; and when any watch is pledged with any pawnbroker, he shall also write in such book the number and name of the maker thereof; and where jewelry, or gold or silver articles of any kind are pledged, he shall note in such book all letters or marks inscribed thereon; and whenever any goods, article or thing of any kind, shall be sold at auction, as hereinafter provided, the date of such sale, the amount for which the same was sold, and the name of the purchaser thereof, shall also be entered in such book.

SEC. 6. Every pawnbroker shall, at the time of making any loan, and receiving any article in pledge therefor, deliver to the person from whom he received it, a memorandum, in writing, signed by him, containing the date and amount of such loan, the rate of interest to be paid thereon, the time within which such article is to be redeemed, with a description of the same, as provided in the preceding section.

SEC. 7. The book provided for in section five of this Ordinance shall, at all times, be open to the inspection of the Mayor or Chief of Police.

Sec. 8. No pawnbroker shall sell any article or thing which may have been left with him in pledge, until the same shall have remained in his possession at least two months beyond the time in which the same was to have been redeemed, and the sale of the same shall be at public auction, after being advertised for at least ten days, in two daily City papers, to be conducted by a licensed auctioneer of the City of Detroit, and not otherwise.

Sec. 9. The surplus money, if any, arising from any sale, as provided in the preceding section, after deducting the amount of the loan, interest and charges due on the same, shall be paid over by such pawnbroker to the person who would have been entitled to redeem such article if no sale had taken place; and if the owner of such surplus money shall not call for the same within one month after such sale, the same shall be paid into the City Treasury.

Sec. 10. It shall be the duty of all pawnbrokers, licensed under this Ordinance, on receiving information that any article or thing left with them in pledge has been lost or stolen, to notify, in writing, the Chief of Police of the fact, giving the name of the person from whom they received the same, and the time when it was received.

Sec. 11. No pawnbroker shall purchase any article or thing offered to him as a pledge.

Sec. 12. No pawnbroker shall receive in pledge any article or thing from any person under sixteen years of age, or who is intoxicated, or an habitual drunkard.

Sec. 13. No pawnbroker shall, knowingly, take from any apprentice, or servant, any article or thing offered by them in pledge, without first ascertaining that such article or thing is the property of the person so offering the same in pledge.

Sec. 14. Any violation of, or failure to comply with the provisions of this Ordinance, shall be punished by a fine not to exceed one hundred dollars and costs; and the offender may be sentenced to be imprisoned, until the payment thereof, in the Detroit House of Correction, for a term not exceeding six months.

TITLE VII.

THE PUBLIC HEALTH.

CHAPTER 70.

BOARD OF HEALTH.

[Chapter Sixty-six of the Revised Ordinances of 1863.]

SECTION 1. The Alderman of each Ward, whose term of office will soonest expire, with two of the City Physicians, and two other physicians, to be designated by a vote of the Common Council, shall be and are hereby constituted a "Board of Health," in and for the City of Detroit, with the powers and duties hereinafter prescribed, and any five of them shall constitute a quorum for the transaction of business. [*As amended by Ordinance approved July 18, 1870.*]

SEC. 2. At their first meeting, which shall be on the third Thursday in January of each year, they shall select from their number a President, who shall hold his office for the term of one year, and in case of vacancy or temporary absence, his place shall be supplied by the election of a President *pro tempore.* [*As amended by Ordinance approved July 18, 1870.*]

SEC. 3. The Board of Health shall meet at the City Hall, and, after their first meeting, at such times as they may deem proper: *Provided,* That the present year the first meeting shall be designated by resolution of the Common Council. The City Clerk shall be the Clerk of the Board of Health, and shall keep regular minutes of their proceedings, in books to be provided for that purpose. [*As amended by Ordinance approved July 18, 1870.*]

SEC. 4. The Board of Health shall have power, and it is hereby made their duty:

1st. To make, and direct to be made, diligent inquiry with respect to all nuisances, of every description, in said City, which are, or may be, injurious to the public health, and abate the same.

2d. To stop, detain and examine, or to direct to be stopped, detained and examined, every person coming from a place infected with a pestilential or infectious disease, in order to prevent the introduction of the same into this City.

3d. To cause any person, not a resident of this City, who is infected with any infectious or pestilential disease, to be sent back to the place from whence he or she came, or to the pest-house or hospital.

4th. To cause any person, a resident of this City, who is infected with any pestilential or infectious disease, to be removed to the pest-house or hospital, if, in the opinion of any two of the City Physicians, the removal of such person is necessary for the preservation of the public health: *Provided, however,* That such removal can be effected with safety to the patient.

5th. To destroy any furniture, wearing apparel, goods, wares, or merchandise, or articles or property of any kind, which shall be exposed to, or infected with a contagious or infectious disease: *Provided, however,* That such property shall be appraised by two disinterested persons, in order that remuneration may be made therefor by the Common Council.

6th. To appoint, with consent of the Common Council, Health Inspectors, with the power and duties hereinafter enumerated.

7th. To rent proper houses, to be used for pest-houses and hospitals.

8th. To employ such nurses, officers, agents servants or assistants, and provide the necessary furniture, medicines, articles and necessaries, for the use of the pest-houses or hospitals, and the persons therein confined as may be deemed necessary.

9th. To require the occupant of any dwelling house, store, shop, or other building in which there shall be any person sick with small-pox, or varioloid, to put up and maintain in a conspicuous place, on the front of said dwelling house, store, shop, or other building, a card or sign, to be furnished by the Board, on which shall be written or printed, in large letters, the words, "SMALL-

Pox," and in case of the neglect or refusal of any person to comply with such requirement, to remove the patient therein to the pest-house or hospital.

10th. To make any order requiring any steamboat, or other vessel or craft, having on board any infected or diseased person or property, not to enter the habor, or to remove therefrom.

11th. To exercise a general supervision over the health of the City, and to make, from time to time, such recommendations to the Common Council as they deem proper, to promote the cleanliness and salubrity of the City.

12th. To make and determine the rules of its own proceedings.

13th. The Board of Health shall annually, and oftener, if they deem it necessary, divide the City into health districts.

14th. The Board of Health shall provide and keep on hand a supply of cards, marked "SMALL-POX," to be put upon any house in which there may be a person sick of that disease or the varioloid; and such cards, upon application, shall be furnished without charge.

15th. Whenever, in their judgment, it shall be necessary for the public health to at once take possession of any building, factory, hotel, dwelling house, out-house, premises or grounds, upon which, in their judgment, there exists any nuisance prejudicial to the public health; and if the owner or occupant shall refuse or neglect to forthwith abate such nuisance, in the manner directed by said Board, said Board may cause the same to be abated forthwith in such manner as they deem proper, and all expenses incurred shall be a legal claim against the owner and a lien upon the premises, to be collected in the same manner as other special assessments. The said Board may also, when they deem it requisite for the public health, at once, and by force, if necessary, close up such houses, buildings, hotels and premises, and exclude all occupants therefrom until such nuisance shall be fully abated and the air of such building or premises is thoroughly purified. Any person who shall resist the action of the Board, or their agents under this subdivision, shall be liable to the penalties provided for in section eighteen of this Chapter. [*As amended by Ordinance approved December 6, 1865.*]

SEC. 5. The keeper of any tavern, boarding or public house, in which any inmate thereof shall be sick with small-pox, varioloid, or other infectious or pestilential disease, shall forthwith report the same to the Board of Health, or to some member, or to the Clerk thereof; and the keeper or keepers aforesaid, if required by the Board, shall close such house immediately, and keep it closed against all lodgers and customers, until the patient is removed, and such house is thoroughly cleansed and ventilated.

SEC. 6. Every physician, or person acting as such, who shall have a patient sick of the small-pox, varioloid, or other infectious and pestilential disease, shall forthwith report the fact, in writing, to the President of the Board of Health, together with the name, and the street and number of the house where such patient is treated; and the President shall report the same at the next meeting of the Board.

SEC. 7. It shall be the duty of the occupant of any dwelling house, or other building, in which there shall be small-pox or varioloid, to put up and maintain, in a conspicuous place, on the front of such building, a card, or sign, to be furnished by the Board of Health, on which shall be written or printed the words, "SMALL-POX," and such sign or card shall be kept on such building during all the time any person so diseased shall remain therein; and no person shall take down, injure or deface such card or sign.

SEC. 8. All persons having small-pox, varioloid, or other contagious or infectious disease, are hereby required to be kept closely confined within their respective dwellings, or places of abode, and no person who has been confined with such disease, shall leave his or her place of abode, and go about the City, until, in the opinion of his or her physician, it can be done without danger of communicating the disease to others.

SEC. 9. No person having the small-pox, varioloid, or other contagious disease, shall go about the City.

SEC. 10. It shall be the duty of each Health Inspector:

1st. To ascertain any nuisance which may exist in his district, and forthwith to report the same, in writing, to the Board.

2d. To enter upon the premises, and into the house of every

person in his district, as often as he shall deem necessary, or the Board of Health shall order, and to examine into the health, cleanliness, and number of persons inhabiting such house, and inspect the cellars, vaults, privies and sewers on such premises.

3d. To execute the orders and resolutions of the Board of Health, in such manner as directed.

SEC. 11. The members of the Board of Health shall be paid one dollar and fifty cents *per diem* for each session of the Board, and they may appoint a Committee on Complaints of Citizens, not to exceed three persons, who shall sit during the day and hear the complaints of citizens. Said committee shall be paid therefor in the discretion of the Board of Health, not to exceed three dollars *per diem.* Said Board shall have the authority to incur such indebtedness as shall be necessary for the proper execution of its powers granted in this Ordinance; all of which, together with the pay of members and committees, shall be submitted to the Common Council for audit and allowance in the same manner as other demands against the City, and shall be paid out of the Contingent Fund, accordingly. [*As amended by Ordinance approved December 12, 1870.*]

SEC. 12. All debts lawfully contracted by the Board of Health, shall be paid by the City, in the same manner that other claims and demands against the City are paid.

SEC. 13. No person shall bring, or cause to be brought into the City of Detroit, any person infected with the small-pox, varioloid, or any other infectious or pestilential disease.

SEC. 14. The Board of Health, through its President, shall, on the first Tuesday in each month, and oftener, if required, make a report to the Common Council, giving any information in their power in respect to the health and salubrity of the City, and also a detailed statement of what money has been expended by them, and for what purpose the same has been expended.

SEC. 15. The pest-houses and hospitals of the City shall be under the control and direction of the Board of Health.

SEC. 16. Whenever property of any description, as enumerated in subdivision five, of section four, shall be destroyed by order of the Board of Health, the same shall be paid for by the

Common Council, like other claims and demands against the Corportion.

SEC. 17. Any violation of, or failure to comply with the provisions of this Ordinance, or failure or neglect to comply with any of the requirements of the Board of Health, shall, on complaint to the Recorder's Court, be punished by a fine not to exceed three hundred dollars, and costs; and in the imposition of any such fine and costs, the Court may make a further sentence, that the offender be imprisoned in the County Jail, or Detroit House of Correction, until such fine and costs be paid: *Provided, however,* That the term of such imprisonment shall not exceed the period of six months.

CHAPTER 71.

SCAVENGERS.

[Chapter Twenty of the Revised Ordinances of 1863.]

SECTION 1. No person shall follow the business or occupation of a Scavenger without a license from the Mayor.

SEC. 2. The Mayor is hereby authorized to license proper persons to act as Scavengers, upon their paying into the City Treasury the sum of one dollar, and executing a bond to the Corporation, with one or more sufficient sureties, conditioned for the faithful observance of the Charter and Ordinances. [*As amended by Ordinance approved December 12, 1870.*]

SEC. 3. Such Scavengers, under the direction of the Mayor, an Alderman, or a member of the Board of Health, shall have the power to enter upon any premises, between sunrise and sunset, and examine any vault, sink, privy or private drain.

SEC. 4. Whenever, in the opinion of the Mayor, an Alderman, or a member of the Board of Health, or Sanitary Policemen, any sink, privy, or private drain shall need cleaning, altering, relaying, or repairing, in order to protect the public health, he shall notify, in writing, the owner or occupant thereof to cause the same to be cleansed, altered, relaid or repaired, within six days from the date of the service of such notice, and in case of the neglect or refusal to comply with the requirement of such notice, the Common Council may direct the proper officer to cleanse, alter, relay or repair such sink, private drain or privy, and assess the expense thereof on the lot or premises attached thereto, which assessment shall be a lien on such lot or premises, and be collected in the same manner as other assessments imposed by authority of the Common Council. [*As amended by Ordinance approved December 12, 1870.*]

SEC. 5. Scavengers shall not empty or remove the contents of any tub, vault, sink, privy, or private drain, otherwise than in boxes or casks, made tight and closely covered; they shall not dispose of such contents to any person or persons who intend to use the same for manure upon any garden or other grounds within the limits of the City of Detroit; and all persons are hereby prohibited from using the contents of any privy for the purpose aforesaid, within the limits of said City; and all persons are hereby expressly prohibited from removing privies from one portion of a lot to another, unless by the written consent of the President of the Board of Health, or of the member of the Board of Health from the Ward in which said removal is proposed, and such consent shall not be given unless the privy, when removed to a new location, shall be thoroughly drained, by connection with a sewer, if practicable, and the old vault emptied of its contents and filled with earth. [*As amended by Ordinance approved March 7, 1868.*]

SEC. 6. When requested, the Scavenger shall cleanse or empty any vault, sink, private drain or privy, and remove any and all nuisances. They may demand and receive their fees for such services in advance.

SEC. 7. The Scavengers shall receive twelve cents for each cubic foot of the contents of any sink, private drain, vault or privy, by them cleaned out or removed; and for removing any dead dog, cat, hog or other animal, or other nuisance, they shall receive such fees as may be, from time to time, fixed by resolution of the Common Council. [*As amended by Ordinance approved June 1, 1866.*]

SEC. 8. Any violation of, or neglect or refusal to comply with, the provisions of this Ordinance, shall be punished by a fine not to exceed fifty dollars and costs of prosecution; and in the imposition of any fine and costs, the court may make a further sentence that the offender be imprisoned until the payment thereof: *Provided,* That the term of such imprisonment shall not exceed the period of six months.

CHAPTER 72.

CEMETERIES.

[Chapter Sixty-seven of the Revised Ordinances of 1863.]

SECTION 1. The Cemeteries known as Elmwood, Mount Elliott, and City Cemetery, are hereby declared to be public burial grounds; and no person or persons, societies or congregations, shall establish or locate any other burying ground within the limits of the City of Detroit.

SEC. 2. No interments shall be made in any other place within the City of Detroit than the Cemeteries hereinbefore named, or such other Cemetery or Cemeteries as may be hereafter established by resolution or Ordinance of the Common Council.

SEC. 3. The grave for an adult shall be at least six feet deep; and for a child at least five feet deep. This section shall apply to all Cemeteries within the City of Detroit.

SEC. 4. No person shall obstruct any walk or alley in the City Cemetery.

SEC. 5. The Common Council shall designate suitable lots in the City Cemetery for the interment of deceased strangers and poor persons.

SEC. 6. On application to the Director of the Poor, with satisfactory proof that the deceased left no means with which to pay funeral expenses, the corpse shall be buried at the expense of the City, and the Director of the Poor shall give an order, commanding the City Sexton to dig a grave, furnish a suitable coffin, place dollars. He may be removed at any time by the Mayor. [*As amended by Ordinance approved April 2, 1863.*]

SEC. 12. The City Sexton, and the Sextons or Superintendents of Elmwood and Mount Elliott Cemeteries, shall each keep a register, to be provided by the City, of all persons buried in each of said Cemeteries, giving in alphabetical order the name of the deceased, age, color, sex, occupation, place of birth and residence, the disease, or manner and time of death, and the number of the lot in which the body was buried; which register shall be kept in the office of the City Clerk. And the Sextons or Superintendents aforesaid, shall, on Monday of each week, in the forenoon, record in the said register, in the manner herein provided, the burials which have been made since their last report.

SEC. 13. No person shall commit any trespass, by destroying, injuring or defacing any grave, vault, tombstone, monument, enclosure, building, fence, basin, fountain, bridge, seat, tree, flower, shrub, or other thing belonging to any Cemetery.

SEC. 14. Any violation of or failure to comply with the provisions of this Ordinance, shall be punished by a fine not to exceed one hundred dollars and costs; and in the imposition of any such fine and costs, the Court may make a further sentence, that in default of the payment thereof, within a time to be fixed in such sentence, the offender be committed to the County Jail or Detroit House of Correction, for any period of time not exceeding six months.

SEC. 15. The City Sexton shall be appointed by the Common Council, on the nomination of the Mayor, and shall hold his office for one year, or until his successor is appointed.

CHAPTER 73.

NUISANCES.

[Chapter Sixty-eight of the Revised Ordinances of 1863.]

SECTION 1. No person, shall, himself, or by another, throw, place, deposit or leave in any street, highway, lane, alley, public space or square, any animal or vegetable substance, dead animal, fish, shells, shavings, dirt, rubbish, excrement, filth, ordure, slops, unclean or nauseous water, liquor or gaseous fluids, hay, straw, ashes, cinders, soot, offal, garbage, swill, or any other article or substance whatever, which may cause any noisome, offensive or unwholesome smell; and all fluids pumped or taken from any of the gas pipes within said City, shall be pumped or conveyed through a hose, or other proper conductor, directly into some public sewer, or in lieu thereof, to be conveyed in a vessel, closely and securely covered, to some public sewer, and the contents emptied therein. [*As amended by Ordinance approved June 2, 1870.*]

SEC. 2. No distiller, dyer, machinist, or other person, shall himself, or by another, discharge out of, or from any still-house, dyehouse, workshop, factory, machine shop, dwelling house, kitchen, or other building, any foul or nauseous liquid, water, or other substance, into or upon any highway, street, lane, alley, public space or square, or into any adjacent lot or ground. No person or persons shall permit on his, her or their premises, within the boundaries of said City, or within a half mile therefrom, of which he or she, or they, may be the occupant or occupants, agent or agents, having charge thereof, a soap or candle factory, or the exercise of any other unwholesome or offensive trade or calling, or suffer any building, sewer or other thing whatsoever to remain on said premises until, in any manner, the same shall become offensive, hurtful, dan-

CHAPTER 73.

NUISANCES.

[Chapter Sixty-eight of the Revised Ordinances of 1863.]

SECTION 1. No person, shall, himself, or by another, throw, place, deposit or leave in any street, highway, lane, alley, public space or square, any animal or vegetable substance, dead animal, fish, shells, shavings, dirt, rubbish, excrement, filth, ordure, slops, unclean or nauseous water, liquor or gaseous fluids, hay, straw, ashes, cinders, soot, offal, garbage, swill, or any other article or substance whatever, which may cause any noisome, offensive or unwholesome smell; and all fluids pumped or taken from any of the gas pipes within said City, shall be pumped or conveyed through a hose, or other proper conductor, directly into some public sewer, or in lieu thereof, to be conveyed in a vessel, closely and securely covered, to some public sewer, and the contents emptied therein. [*As amended by Ordinance approved June 2, 1870.*]

SEC. 2. No distiller, dyer, machinist, or other person, shall himself, or by another, discharge out of, or from any still-house, dye-house, workshop, factory, machine shop, dwelling house, kitchen, or other building, any foul or nauseous liquid, water, or other substance, into or upon any highway, street, lane, alley, public space or square, or into any adjacent lot or ground. No person or persons shall permit on his, her or their premises, within the boundaries of said City, or within a half mile therefrom, of which he or she, or they, may be the occupant or occupants, agent or agents, having charge thereof, a soap or candle factory, or the exercise of any other unwholesome or offensive trade or calling, or suffer any building, sewer or other thing whatsoever to remain on said premises until, in any manner, the same shall become offensive, hurtful, dangerous, or unwholesome to the neighborhood or travelers. [*As amended by Ordinance approved February 8, 1868.*]

SEC. 3. No person shall keep, place, or have, on or in any private house, lot or premises in this City, or within one mile distant therefrom, any dead carcass, putrid, offensive, or unsound beef, pork, fish, hides, skins, bones, horns, stinking or rotten soap grease, tallow offal, garbage, or other animal or vegetable matter or substance which may cause any unwholesome, noisome or offensive smell.

SEC. 4. When any dumb animal shall die within the limits of the City of Detroit, the owner, or person in possession of it, shall, within twelve hours thereafter, cause the carcass to be removed to the place provided by the Common Council, or one mile beyond the City limits.

SEC. 5. No owner or occupant of any grocery, cellar, tallow-chandler's shop, soap, candle, starch or glue factory, tannery, butcher shop, slaughter house, stable, barn, privy, sewer, or other building or place, shall allow any nuisance to exist or remain on his or her premises.

SEC. 6. The keeper of any livery or other stable shall keep the stable and stable yard clean, and shall not permit, between the first day of June and the first day of November, more than two cart-loads of manure to accumulate in or near the same, at any one time.

SEC. 7. No person shall, himself, or by another, wash or clean any carriage or horse, on any street, sidewalk, or other public space, nor suffer the water used for such purposes to flow over any sidewalk, street or public space.

SEC. 8. Every person slaughtering beeves, sheep, or other animals, within the City limits, shall cause the house, yard or place where such killing is done, to be provided with a tight plank floor, or to be paved with brick or stone; and, if paved, the earth below shall be sufficiently solid to prevent its becoming the receptacle of the filthy or offensive matter; such floor or pavement shall be so constructed as to carry off into a tub or reservoir all blood and offal. At the end of each day, when killing has been done on the premises, and at the end of each day when, for any other cause, any blood, offal, or other offensive material or garbage, shall have accumulated on the premises, the occupant shall cause the premises to be thoroughly washed and cleansed, and shall also cause the contents of said tubs, vessels or reservoirs, and all other offal, garbage and offensive matter on the premises, to be conveyed to some place without the City limits, and no such occupant shall suffer or permit the contents of such tubs or vessels, or such offal, garbage or offensive matter, to be emptied into any public or private drain or sewer within the City limits. [*As amended by Ordinance approved June 1, 1866.*]

SEC. 9. Every slaughter house in this City shall be whitewashed inside, at least once in each month, between the first day of April and the first day of November.

SEC. 10. No person shall allow any green or salted hides to remain on any street, sidewalk, or other open place within this City, longer than one hour.

SEC. 11. No person shall, himself, or by another, post or put up in any conspicuous place, or on any of the lamp posts, fences, posts, hydrants, boxes, sidewalks, bridges or buildings within this City, any card or handbill, advertising the place or means of curing syphilitic or other secret diseases.

SEC. 12. Hereafter, no person shall, himself, or by another, post, attach, place, print, paint or stamp any placard, show-bill or advertisement of any description whatever (except such as may be expressly authorized by law), on any street or sidewalk, or on any other public place or object in the City, or on any fence or inclosure belonging to the City. It shall be the duty of the police of said City to see to the enforcement of this Ordinance, and to make complaint against any persons violating the provisions thereof. [*As amended by Ordinance approved July 5, 1867.*]

SEC. 13. No person, or persons, shall collect or confine hogs, cows or cattle, in herds, pens, enclosures, or otherwise, so as to become offensive to his, her, or their neighbor, or neighbors, in any locality within the limits of the City of Detroit. [*As amended by Ordinance approved August 5, 1864.*]

SEC. 14. No person shall place, deposit, throw or keep, in any dock or wharf, or in the waters of the Detroit River, within the

City limits, any straw, hay, green boughs, manure, cord-wood, vegetables, perishable substance, excrement, carcass, bones, horns, shells, meats, hides, offals, garbage, or any unwholesome or decayed matter or thing whatever.

SEC. 15. Every dwelling house, store, manufactory, or shop hereafter built in the City of Detroit, shall be provided with a suitable privy, the vault of which shall be walled up with two-inch plank, brick or stone, and be sunk at least four feet below the level of the earth. The inside of such vault shall be at least one foot distant from the line of every adjoining highway, street, lane, alley or lot; and when there is a public sewer within one hundred feet of such privy, it shall be so constructed as to be drained into such sewer.

SEC. 16. The Mayor, Aldermen of the City, and members of the Board of Health, shall have the power, and it is hereby made their and each of their duty, upon being satisfied that any store, manufactory, shop, or dwelling house, as aforesaid, is not provided with a suitable privy, as provided in the last section, to notify, in writing, the owner or occupant of such dwelling to construct such a privy within twenty days from the date of the service of such notice; and if such owner or occupant neglect or refuse to comply with the requirements of such notice, within the time specified, the Common Council may cause a suitable privy to be constructed for such dwelling house, and the expense thereof shall be charged as a special tax or assessment on the dwelling house, and the ground attached thereto, to be levied and collected in the same manner as other assessments imposed by authority of the Common Council.

SEC. 17. No privy shall be emptied between the fifteenth day of June and the fifteenth day of September, unless by the written permission of the Mayor, an Alderman, or a member of the Board of Health. Privies shall be emptied between the hours of 10 P. M., and 3 A. M., and at no other time.

SEC. 18. Any cart, wagon or other vehicle, used or intended to be used for the purpose of conveying swill, offal, garbage, excrement, ordure or night-soil, shall be perfectly tight and covered, so as to prevent the contents thereof from leaking or spilling;

and such cart, wagon or other vehicle, when not in use, shall not be allowed to stand in any highway, street, lane, alley, public space or square.

SEC. 19. Any violation of the provisions of this Ordinance, shall be punished by a fine not to exceed one hundred dollars, and the costs of prosecution; and in the imposition of any fine and costs, the Court may make a further sentence, that the offender be imprisoned in the Wayne County Jail or the Detroit House of Correction, until the payment thereof: *Provided, however,* That the period of such imprisonment shall not exceed the term of six months.

CHAPTER 74.

REMOVAL OF GARBAGE, ETC.

[Ordinance approved June 1, 1866.]

SECTION 1. It is hereby made the duty of the occupant or occupants of every dwelling house or other building in the City of Detroit, to provide a suitable and tight box, or other vessel, in which such occupant or occupants shall cause to be placed or deposited all the offal, garbage and kitchen refuse of the premises; such occupant or occupants shall also cause the contents of such box or vessel to be taken, twice in each week, from the first of May to the first of November, and once in each week from the first of November to the first of May, in each year, to some place without the limits of the City, and to be there deposited.

SEC. 2. The Common Council, upon the nomination of the Chairman of the Board of Health, shall appoint one person in each Ward of the City, who shall be known and called the "Ward Officer for the — Ward," whose duty it shall be to see that the foregoing provisions are complied with. It shall also be the duty of said officer, whenever he has any knowledge of the non-compliance with said foregoing provisions, to enter a complaint against the person offending. It shall also be the duty of said officer to make inspection of any premises between the hours of 8 A. M. and 4 P. M., whenever he finds that any offal, garbage, or other offensive matter is not removed, in compliance with the foregoing provisions, to enter upon the premises, and to remove the same. And such officer is hereby authorized to so enter and remove.

SEC. 3. Whenever such officer shall so enter upon premises, and remove offal, garbage, or other offensive matter, under the last preceding section, he shall be entitled to demand, and receive of and from the occupant or occupants of the premises, the sum of three cents, and it shall be the duty of such occupant or occupants to pay him the same, upon demand, for each and every such entry and removal.

SEC. 4. Any person failing or neglecting to comply with the requirements of this Ordinance shall be subject to prosecution in the Recorder's Court, and upon conviction shall be subject to punishment by fine not exceeding four dollars, or by imprisonment in the House of Correction not exceeding two days.

SEC. 5. The Ward Officers shall be entitled to, and shall receive no compensation from the City of Detroit.

CHAPTER 75.

SLAUGHTER HOUSES.

[Ordinance approved December 27, 1864.]

SECTION 1. No person shall slaughter, or cause to be slaughtered, in any building or enclosure on either side of Jefferson avenue, Woodward avenue, and Fort street west, or within one block of each of said avenues or said street, any cattle, sheep, swine or calves.

SEC. 2. Any violation of the provisions of this Ordinance shall be punished by a fine not to exceed three hundred dollars, and costs; and in the imposition of any fine and costs, the court may make a further sentence, that the offender be committed to the Detroit House of Correction, or County Jail, until such fine and costs be paid: *Provided, however,* that the term of such imprisonment shall not exceed the period of six months.

CHAPTER 76.

REMOVAL AND BURIAL OF DEAD ANIMALS.

[Ordinance approved April 2, 1870.]

SECTION 1. That the City of Detroit is hereby divided into two districts, to be called Dog Scavenger Districts, as follows: All that portion of the City of Detroit lying east of the center of Woodward avenue, shall constitute and be known as the Eastern Dog Scavenger District; and all that portion of said City lying west of the center of Woodward avenue, shall constitute and be known as the Western Dog Scavenger District.

SEC. 2. It shall be the duty of the Controller, on the first of March in each year, or as soon thereafter as directed by the Common Council, to advertise for proposals for the removal and burial of all dead animals, as provided in this Ordinance, and the contracts therefor shall be let to the lowest responsible bidder: *Provided, however,* That said contracts shall be let separately for the Eastern and Western Districts.

SEC. 3. It shall be the duty of the members of the Metropolitan Police force to report to the Station House each day, any dead animal discovered by them within the limits of the City.

SEC. 4. It shall be the duty of any person or persons to whom a contract may be let under this Ordinance, during the months of June, July, August and September, on each day, to apply to the different police stations, or any other proper place that may from time to time be designated by the Common Council or Board of Health, at the hours of 7 A. M. and 1 P. M., and during the other eight months of the year at 9 o'clock A. M., and ascertain what dead animals, if any, are reported to be lying anywhere within the limits of the City since his last application, and if any are so reported the contractor shall forthwith proceed to remove and bury such animals, as provided in this Ordinance; and it shall also be the duty of said contractor to forthwith remove, in the manner prescribed in this Ordinance, any dead animal that may be reported to him by any citizen, or any dead animal within the limits of the City that said contractor may discover without such notice as aforesaid.

SEC. 5. Whenever notice is brought to the knowledge of the contractor that the carcass of any animal is lying anywhere within the limits of the City, the contractor or contractors shall at once cause the same to be removed in a tight box, securely covered, placed in a wagon or cart, to be furnished by him or them, to some suitable place at least one mile beyond the limits of the City, and to bury said carcass in such manner as to cause it to be covered with at least three feet of solid earth from the level of the ground where such carcass is buried.

SEC. 6. The contractor or contractors shall furnish all necessary conveyances for the removal of any carcasses under this Ordinance, and shall also furnish the ground or grounds where said carcasses shall be deposited.

SEC. 7. The contractor or contractors for performing said services shall be paid each month one-twelfth of the contract price, in the same manner as other accounts are audited and allowed.

SEC. 8. The contractor or contractors in entering upon a contract under this Ordinance shall be required to file bonds to the amount of five hundred dollars, for the faithful performance of any work herein mentioned.

SEC. 9. In case any contractor fails to comply with the conditions of this Ordinance, he shall be liable to prosecution in the Recorder's Court and subject to a fine not to exceed twenty dollars and the costs of prosecution, or imprisonment in the Detroit House of Correction for any period not exceeding six months.

SEC. 10. This Ordinance shall take immediate effect.

TITLE VIII.

THE PUBLIC PEACE.

CHAPTER 77.

POLICE JUSTICE.

[Ordinance Approved December 21, 1870.]

SECTION 1. It shall be the duty of the Police Justice to attend the City Hall or any other Police Station House where the lock-up shall be, on every day of the week, Sundays excepted, at the hour of seven A. M. from the first day of April to the first day of November, and at the hour of eight A. M. from the first day of November to the first day of April; he shall summarily examine into the case of every person confined in said station house, and if he adjudge any person guilty of vagrancy, disorderly conduct or any violation of City Ordinances, relative to breaches of the peace, drunken persons or mendicants, he may convict such person or persons thereof, and commit him or her to the Wayne County Jail, or to the Detroit House of Correction, for not more than six months, and impose a fine not exceeding fifty dollars, and in default of the immediate payment thereof, to commit such person or persons to the Wayne County Jail, or to the Detroit House of Correction, for a term not exceeding six months, or until such fine be paid.

SEC. 2. The Police Justice shall receive for his services in performing the duties required by the foregoing section, the sum of six hundred dollars per annum.

SEC. 3. It shall be the duty of the Clerk of the Police Court to attend the City Hall, or any other Police Station House where the lock-up shall be, on every day of the week, Sundays excepted, at the hour of 7 o'clock A. M. from the first day of April to the first day of November, and at the hour of eight A. M. from the first day of November to the first day of April, to keep a true record of the proceedings before the Police Justice at said station, in proper books to be provided therefor, and file and safely keep all papers pertaining to such proceedings; it shall be his duty to receive all costs, fines and dues of every description, from either party to complaints or prosecutions, before said Police Justice, and which by law, are taxable as Justice's costs, and shall pay the same weekly to the City Treasurer, and take his receipt therefor.

SEC. 4. Said Clerk shall receive as compensation for performing the duties specified in section 3, the sum of two hundred dollars per annum.

CHAPTER 78.

THE PUBLIC PEACE.

[Ordinance approved April 7, 1870.]

SECTION 1. All able-bodied persons, who, not having visible means of support, are found loitering or rambling about, or lodging or loitering in drinking saloons, tippling houses, beer houses, houses of ill-fame, houses of bad repute, vessels, sheds or barns, or in the open air, and not giving good account of themselves, or begging in the street or elsewhere, all keepers or exhibitors of any gaming table or device, and all persons who, for the purpose of gaming, or for the purpose of watch-stuffing, travel about or go from place to place, and all persons upon whom shall be found any instrument or thing used for the commission of burglary, larceny, or for picking locks or pockets, or anything used for obtaining money under false pretenses, and who cannot give a good account of their possession of the same, and all fortune-tellers, shall be deemed vagrants, and upon conviction thereof, shall be punished by a fine not exceeding fifty dollars, and in default of the immediate payment thereof, shall be committed to the Detroit House of Correction, until such fine be paid: *Provided*, Such time of imprisonment shall not exceed the period of six months.

SEC. 2. Any person or persons who shall make or assist in making any noise, disturbance, or improper diversion, or any rout or riot, by which the peace and good order of the neighborhood are disturbed, or shall be guilty of disorderly conduct, shall be punished as hereinafter provided.

SEC. 3. No person shall be guilty of any indecent or immoral language, conduct or behavior to any person in any public street, lane, alley, square, park or space in said City.

SEC. 4. All mendicants and drunken persons shall be punished as hereinafter provided.

SEC. 5. Any person, who shall, by talking, laughing, or otherwise, interrupt the service in any place of Divine worship, shall be punished as hereinafter provided.

SEC. 6. Persons shall not collect or stand in crowds, in front of any church or place of worship, during service, or the gathering and departing of the congregation.

SEC. 7. No person shall make any indecent exposure of his or her person in the streets, lanes, alleys, markets, or public places of said City.

SEC. 8. No person shall show, sell, or offer for sale or exhibit, any indecent or obscene picture, drawing, engraving, book or pamphlet.

SEC. 9. Any violations of the provisions of this Ordinance, shall be punished by a fine not to exceed fifty dollars; and in the imposition of any fine, the Court may make a further sentence, that the offender be committed to the Detroit House of Correction or County Jail until such fine be paid: *Provided, however*, That the term of such imprisonment shall not exceed the period of six months.

CHAPTER 79.

DISORDERLY HOUSES.

[Chapter Seventy-one of the Revised Ordinances of 1863.]

SECTION 1. No person shall keep, within the limits of the City of Detroit, any house of ill-fame, house of assignation, or house for the resort of common prostitutes, or a disorderly saloon, bar-room, tavern, beer hall, grocery, theatre, room, ordinary, house or building of any kind.

SEC. 2. Any person who shall violate the preceding section, shall be punished by a fine not to exceed one hundred dollars, and costs of prosecution, and the offender may be sentenced to be imprisoned in the House of Correction until the payment thereof: *Provided, however,* That the term of such imprisonment shall not exceed six months.

CHAPTER 80.

IMPRISONMENT OF OFFENDERS.

[Chapter Seventy-six of the Revised Ordinances of 1863.]

SECTION 1. Whenever, by the terms of any Ordinance of said City it is provided that any person convicted of an offense, shall be imprisoned, said person may be confined either in the County Jail of the County of Wayne, or in any Jail, Workhouse, House of Correction, or Alms House of said City, in the discretion of the Court.

CHAPTER 81.

PRESERVATION OF PUBLIC PROPERTY.

[Chapter Seventy-three of the Revised Ordinances of 1863.]

SECTION 1. No person shall destroy, injure, or in any manner deface the City Hall, the Market Houses, water pipes, water screws, hydrants, public school buildings, fire engine houses, fire apparatus, hay scales, public pounds, public wharves, street lamps, lamp posts, or any public building or property whatsoever, in the City of Detroit, or the appurtenances, fences, trees, or fixtures, thereunto belonging or appertaining.

SEC. 2. No person shall injure any public reservoir or, break, or enter the same, or throw or deposit any substance therein, or draw off any water therefrom, except in case of fire, or for the use of the Fire Department, without authority from the Common Council, the Mayor of the City, or Chief Engineer of the Fire Department.

SEC. 3. No person shall destroy, cut, or injure, or in any way deface any shade or ornamental tree, standing in any street, avenue, public space, or square, in the City of Detroit. This section shall not be construed to prohibit any person, owning or occupying any lot, in front of, or adjacent to, which there may be any shade or ornamental trees, from trimming the same.

SEC. 4. Any person violating any of the provisions of this Ordinance, shall be punished by a fine not to exceed the sum of five hundred dollars, and costs, and the offender may be sentenced to be imprisoned in the Detroit House of Correction until the payment thereof, for a term not exceeding six months.

CHAPTER 82.

CARE OF WATER PIPES, ETC.

[Ordinance approved June 17, 1864.]

SECTION 1. It shall be the duty of each and every person who may, while excavating in any public street or alley, have in any manner contributed to create a leak, or discover any leak or defect, in any of the public water pipes of the City, or in any service pipe, connected therewith, to give notice forthwith to the contractor, superintendent or overseer of the work in process of excavation, whose duty it shall be forthwith to give notice thereof to the Secretary of the Board of Water Commissioners.

SEC. 2. No person shall fill up such excavation, or suffer or cause the same to be filled up, until such pipe is repaired and such leak stopped.

SEC. 3. No person shall, save for the purpose of extinguishing fires, open any street reservoir or cistern, or fire hydrant, or use any water from the same, without having first procured the special permission of the Fire Marshal or of the Secretary of the Board of Water Commissioners.

SEC. 4. Any person who shall willfully offend against the provisions of this Ordinance, shall be punished by a fine not exceeding two dollars and costs.

TITLE IX.

THE RECORDER'S COURT.

CHAPTER 83.

PROCEEDINGS.

[Ordinance approved March 28, 1870.]

SECTION 1. Upon complaint, on oath, or affirmation, being made to the Clerk of the Recorder's Court, that any person has violated any of the Laws or Ordinances of said City, the Clerk shall issue a warrant for the arrest of such person, which warrant shall be returnable on the first and third Mondays of each term.

SEC. 2. Before issuing such process, the Clerk may, if he shall deem it necessary, require the complainant to enter into a bond, with sufficient surety, to the City of Detroit, conditioned for the appearance of the complainant at the term of the Recorder's Court at which such process shall be made returnable, to give evidence against the persons complained of by him; and if, upon trial, the defendant shall be discharged, that the complainant shall pay the costs of prosecution, if so ordered by the said Court. And in his discretion said Clerk may require a sum not exceeding five dollars to be deposited with him by the complainant, to be applied to the payment of the costs, in case the complainant is so ordered to pay the same.

SEC. 3. It shall be the duty of a member of the Metropolitan Police force to serve all warrants issued by said Clerk, and to forthwith arrest and bring before said Clerk the person named in said warrant, if he be found, who shall thereupon give bail before said Clerk for his appearance at the Recorder's Court on the return day mentioned in said warrant; and in case any person shall not furnish the required bail, he shall be committed to the Wayne County Jail to await his trial.

SEC. 4. The bail required in the preceding section shall be by bond, payable to the City of Detroit, with such surety as the Clerk may deem necessary, in a sum not less than fifty dollars, and not more than double the amount of the penalty provided in the By-Law or Ordinance which may be violated, and shall be conditioned for the due appearance of the defendant before the Recorder's Court, at the time such warrant shall be returnable, and that the defendant shall comply with the judgment of the Recorder's Court, and not depart without leave, and, in the meantime, keep the peace toward all the people of said City: *Provided*, That if such bail should be insufficient or irresponsible, the officer taking the same shall be liable in an action of debt, for the amount thereof, to be recovered in the name of the Corporation.

SEC. 5. Executions returnable at the next term, may issue upon any judgment of the said Court, against the body, goods and chattels of the defendant, or party prosecuted (unless such party be in actual custody for the offense on which judgment was rendered), for the amount of such fine, and the costs of prosecution, which execution may be levied upon the goods and chattels, or body of such party, and all goods and chattels so levied upon, shall be sold in the same manner, in all respects, that personal property is directed by the laws of the State to be sold, except that six days previous notice of sale shall be sufficient, and the officer levying the same shall return the execution at the next term of the Recorder's Court, with doings thereon. And if such execution be returned unsatisfied, in whole or in part, an execution may be issued against the real estate of such defendant, which shall be executed according to the laws of this State.

SEC. 6. If, in any trial, it shall appear to the Court, that the complaint was willful or malicious, or without probable cause, or if the complainant does not appear and testify in the cause, the Court may order and adjudge the complainant (and if he has entered in a bond, as required by this Ordinance, then him and his surety), to pay the costs of such prosecution, and thereupon an execution, as in other cases, shall issue for the same. But if a deposit in money has been made, such costs shall be paid therefrom, and no execution shall issue. In all cases the surplus of any money deposited for costs, after the payment of such costs, shall be returned by said Clerk to the complainant.

SEC. 7. The City Attorney shall collect all fines, costs and penalties that are imposed for the violation of any Ordinance of said City, in said Court, and he shall immediately pay over to the City Treasurer all moneys by him received, belonging to the Corporation, and shall take from the Treasurer a receipt therefor, which, when presented to, and countersigned by the Controller, shall be a sufficient voucher to said Attorney for such payments, and shall make a return of the same to the Common Council.

SEC. 8. The Clerk of the Recorder's Court shall keep a record, in books to be provided for that purpose, of all proceedings had for the violation of City Ordinances, together with the amount of fines, costs, and penalties imposed in each case, and at the close of each term of the Recorder's Court, he shall report to the Common Council the amount of all fines, costs, and penalties imposed during said term, for the violation of any Ordinances of said City.

SEC. 9. Whenever any person is convicted, before the Recorder's Court, of any offense against the Ordinances of said City, it shall be competent for the Court to require from the party so convicted a recognizance, with sufficient surety or sureties, in such sum as the Court shall direct, conditioned for his or her good behavior for any period not exceeding one year, and any violation of the Ordinance under which the party was convicted, shall be deemed a breach of such recognizance. The Court may also order such party to be committed to the House of Correction till such recognizance be given.

SEC. 10. Whenever any vacancy shall hereafter occur in the said office of Recorder of said City, the same shall be filled for the unexpired portion of the official term at the next annual City election thereafter, if sufficient time intervene to give the notice required by law: *Provided*, That if such time does not intervene, or if such vacancy occurs more than three months prior to the next ensuing annual City election, the Common Council may, in its discretion, order a special election to fill such vacancy for the residue of the official term.

CHAPTER 84.

COSTS.

[Ordinance approved April 11, 1870.]

SECTION 1. In all cases where a person shall be convicted in the Recorder's Court of the City of Detroit of a violation of any City Ordinance, or of any offense against the Charter of said City, the said Court may require the party so convicted to pay the costs of prosecution.

SEC. 2. The costs of prosecution shall be taxed by the Clerk of said Court, as follows: For drawing each complaint, fifty cents; for drawing each warrant, fifty cents; for serving each warrant, fifty cents; for drawing each recognizance, fifty cents; for drawing each original subpœna, and affixing the seal of the Court thereon, and for serving copies thereof, fifty cents each; for drawing each mittimus, one dollar; and for jury fees, where a jury trial is demanded, five dollars: *Provided*, The Court may, in its discretion, remit any or all the costs herein specified.

TITLE X.

PREVENTION OF FIRES.

CHAPTER 85.

PREVENTION OF FIRES.

[Chapter eighty-one of the Revised Ordinances of 1863.]

SECTION 1. The following boundaries shall constitute and be known as the Fire Limits of the City of Detroit, to wit: Beginning at the channel bank of the Detroit River, on the easterly line of the Rivard farm (so called); thence northerly, on said easterly line, to a point within one hundred (100) feet of the south line of Jefferson avenue; thence easterly parallel with said avenue, and one hundred (100) feet therefrom, to the east line of the B. Chapaton farm; thence northerly across said avenue, on the east line of the B. Chapaton farm, to a point one hundred (100) feet north of the northerly line of Jefferson avenue; thence west, parallel with said Jefferson avenue, and one hundred (100) feet therefrom, to Dequindre street; thence northerly, on the west line of Dequindre street to a point 130 feet north of the north line of Larned street; thence west, parallel with said Larned street, and one hundred and thirty (130) feet therefrom, to the easterly line of Rivard farm; thence northerly, on said easterly line, to an alley between Fort and Lafayette streets; thence west on a line with the center of said alley, to the easterly side line of St. Antoine street; thence northerly along the easterly line of St. Antoine street, to Gratiot street; thence easterly along the rear lines of all lots fronting or touching the southerly line of Gratiot street, to the center of Russell street; thence northerly, on the center of Russell street, to a point one hundred

(100) feet distant, at right angles from the northerly line of Gratiot street; thence southwesterly, and parallel with Gratiot street, one hundred (100) feet therefrom, to the easterly side line of lot No. 172, on the corner of Gratiot and Prospect streets; thence northerly on the side line of said lot, to the rear line of the same; thence southwesterly, along the rear lines of all lots fronting on or touching the northerly line of Gratiot street, to a point one hundred (100) feet east of Brush street; thence north, parallel with said Brush street, and one hundred (100) feet distant therefrom, to an alley between Adams avenue and Elizabeth street; thence west, on a line with the center of said alley, to a point one hundred feet distant from the easterly line of Woodward avenue; thence northerly, parallel with said Woodward avenue, and one hundred (100) feet distant therefrom, to a point one hundred (100) feet beyond Charlotte street; thence across Woodward avenue, parallel with Charlotte street, to a point one hundred (100) feet west of the westerly line of Woodward avenue; thence southerly, parallel with said avenue, one hundred (100) feet distant therefrom, to the center of an alley between Adams avenue and Elizabeth street; thence westerly, on the center of said alley, to the center of Clifford street; thence southerly to the northerly line of Middle street; thence westerly to the northerly line of Grand River Road; thence northwesterly, to the westerly line of Cass avenue; thence northerly to the rear line of the lots fronting on Grand River Road; thence northwesterly, along the rear lines of all lots fronting on said Grand River Road, to a point one hundred (100) feet northwest to the west line of Third street; thence south, parallel with Third street, to the rear line of the lot fronting on the south line of the Grand River Road; thence southeasterly, along the rear line of all lots fronting on said road, to a point one hundred (100) feet west of the west line of Cass street; then southerly, in the alley in rear of Cass street, to the southerly line of lot No. 2, block 54; thence easterly, between said lot 2 and lot 3, to the westerly side line of Cass street; thence in a straight line across Cass street, to the middle of an alley between lots 72 and 34; thence through said alley to the easterly side line of lot 34; thence southerly, between lots 33 and 34,

in block 12, to Macomb avenue; thence across said avenue, to the dividing line between lots 33 and 34, block 10; thence southerly, between said lots 33 and 34, and between 72 and 73, to West Park place; thence across said West Park place, to the dividing line between lots 60 and 61 in said block 10; thence on the dividing line between said lots 60 and 61, to the alley between Park place and Washington avenue; thence southerly, in said alley, to an alley eighty (80) feet southerly from Michigan avenue; thence along said alley, adjoining the lots fronting on Michigan avenue, to an alley one hundred (100) feet westerly from Cass street; thence west, along the rear lines of all lots fronting on said avenue, to the easterly line of Sixteenth street; thence southerly, to the rear line of lots fronting on the south line of Michigan avenue; thence along said rear line of all lots fronting on Michigan avenue, to a point one hundred (100) feet west of the westerly line of Third street; thence southerly, parallel with Third street, and one hundred (100) feet therefrom, to an alley one hundred and thirty (130) feet distant north from the north line of Lafayette avenue; thence westerly on a line parallel with said avenue, to a point one hundred (100) feet distant from the west line of Twelfth street; thence south, and parallel with Twelfth street, to a point one hundred and thirty-eight (138) feet south of the southerly line of Fort street; thence easterly, and parallel with Fort street, one hundred and thirty-eight (138) feet therefrom, to the easterly side line of the Forsyth farm (so-called); thence southerly to the channel bank of the Detroit river. It is to be understood that in all reference to the line of lots, those shown on Monroe's City map are those referred to. [*As amended by Ordinance approved December 9, 1870.*]

SEC. 2. No person shall erect or place any building, or part of any building, within said Fire Limits, unless the same shall be constructed of stone, brick or iron, roofs covered with slate, tile, metal, gravel and composition, or shingles laid on not less than five-eighths inches of mortar, and cornices of stone, brick, metal or wood; and if wood, the same shall be painted with three coats of paint, and heavily sanded; the gutters shall be of metal. And in all buildings erected of stone, brick or iron, in blocks of two or more buildings, within said Fire Limits, there shall be erected partition walls of stone or brick, at least one foot in thickness, where such building is over two stories in height, and not less than eight inches in thickness where such building is two stories, or less, in height; and all party and side walls, in such blocks, shall extend at least twenty inches above the roof.

Sec. 3. The Common Council may, by resolution, authorize the erection of wooden buildings within said Fire Limits, under such restrictions, and upon such conditions, as they may prescribe by resolution: *Provided,* That the erection of such wooden building will not increase the fire risk of any building adjacent thereto.

Sec. 4. No person shall, within said Fire Limits, except as provided in section six, repair any wooden building which has been partially destroyed by fire, or otherwise, nor elevate from the ground, or in any way increase the height of, nor remove any such building from one lot to another lot, or to any part of the same lot, without being first authorized to do so by the Common Council.

Sec. 5. When any wooden building within the Fire Limits shall be partially destroyed by fire, or otherwise, and the damage thereto shall not exceed one-third its value, to be ascertained in the manner hereinafter provided, such building may be repaired, and not otherwise; and the Fire Marshal shall give a written permit to such owner, to repair such building, and shall keep a record of the same in his office.

Sec. 6. In case of the partial destruction by fire, or otherwise, of any wooden building in said Fire Limits, the Fire Marshal, and in case of his absence, or inability to act, then the City Controller, with a master builder, to be selected by the owner of such building; and if the building be insured, a third party, to be selected by the Insurance Company, or its agent; and if there be more than one Insurance Company having risks upon such building, then such Insurance Companies, or their agents, shall, together, select such third person, who shall proceed at once to estimate the amount of the damage to such building. But if the Insurance Companies, or their agents, shall neglect or refuse to act, or if there be no insurance on such building, and the Fire

Marshal, and the person selected by the owner of such building, cannot agree as to the amount of such damage, they shall call in a third disinterested person, and the estimate of any two of the parties hereinbefore named, shall be binding on the City, as well as on the owner, and all other persons interested in such building.

SEC. 7. In estimating the value of any building partially destroyed by fire, or otherwise, the sum of money it would cost to build the same new, from the bottom of the sills, shall be taken as its value; and in estimating the damage to such building, the same shall be assumed to be the sum of money it would require to restore such building to the condition in which it was before its partial destruction.

SEC. 8. On the application, in writing, of the owner or owners of two-thirds of the ground in any block not included within the Fire Limits, the Common Council may, by resolution, passed by a two-thirds vote of the Aldermen present, extend to such block the provisions of this Ordinance. A block shall be construed to mean a space bounded by three or more streets.

SEC. 9. Every resolution for the extension of the Fire Limits, as provided in the last section, shall be published for six successive days in the official newspaper of the City, and in one other daily newspaper published in said City.

SEC. 10. For each and every week which a building erected, placed, removed, or repaired, contrary to the provisions of this Ordinance, shall be allowed to remain, the owner of such building may be complained of as for a distinct offense, and punished as hereinafter provided.

SEC. 11. No person shall, without permission of the Common Council, use or occupy, within the limits of the City of Detroit, any building for the manufacture of turpentine, camphene, lime, fireworks, or other dangerous or easily inflammable or explosive substances, or for the storage of gunpowder, in larger quantities than twenty-eight pounds, or for the storage of fireworks of any description whatever. [*As amended by Ordinance approved June 18, 1870.*]

SEC. 12. No person shall have, put or keep any hay, straw, cotton, hemp or wood shavings, in stack or pile, without having the same securely enclosed, so as to protect them from flying sparks of fire.

SEC. 13. No lighted candle or lamp shall be used in any stable, building, or other place where hay, straw, hemp, cotton, flax, rushes, shavings, gunpowder, or other combustible materials shall be stowed or lodged, unless the same is well secured in a lantern.

SEC. 14. Every chimney hereafter erected within the limits of the City, shall be so constructed as to admit of being scraped, brushed or cleansed.

SEC. 15. No pipe of any stove, chimney or fireplace, shall be put up or used, unless the same be conducted into a chimney of stone or brick; and in all cases where a stove pipe passes through the woodwork of a building, it shall be separated from such woodwork at least six inches, by metal or other incombustible material; and all pipes from stoves or fire-places, over fifteen feet in length, shall be riveted together at each joint, and, when necessary for safety, shall be supported and stayed by wires.

SEC. 16. It shall be the duty of the person or persons occupying or using any building within the limits of the City of Detroit, to cause all chimneys which may be used therein to be swept or scraped out once in every twelve months; and it shall be the duty of the City Chimney Sweeper, or his authorized agent, once in every twelve months, to inspect all chimneys in use in the City of Detroit, and if any of said chimneys have not been swept or scraped out at any time within the period of twelve months, as aforesaid, the said City Chimney Sweeper shall forthwith cause said chimney or chimneys to be cleaned and swept out, and the occupant of such premises shall pay or cause to be paid to said City Chimney Sweeper, upon the completion of said work, the following sums, and no more: For each chimney with a single flue, the sum of twenty-five cents for every story through which such flue shall pass, and for each additional flue ten cents. [*As amended by Ordinance approved April 2, 1870.*]

SEC. 17. No person shall carry fire in or through any street, alley or lot in this City, unless the same be placed in some covered pan or vessel.

SEC. 18. No ashes shall be kept or deposited in any part of this

City, unless the same be kept or deposited in a close iron or earthen vessel, or brick or stone ash house, thoroughly secured.

SEC. 19. No person shall kindle any fire, or furnish the materials for any fire, to be made or kindled in any street, alley or vacant place, within the thickly populated portions of this City, unless for the purpose of boiling tar, pitch or oil, to be used in the construction or repair of some building or vessel.

SEC. 20. No person shall fire or set off any squib, cracker, gunpowder, or fireworks, or fire any cannon, gun or pistol, in any street, lane or alley, or in any yard, public or private, within the limits of the City, unless by a written permission from the Mayor; and such permission shall specify the object, and limit the time of such firing: *Provided,* That, save in the case of using or firing any gun or pistol, which are expressly prohibited, this Section shall not be extended to the prohibition of the usual demonstrations on the 4th of July, the 22d of February, the 1st of January, and the 17th day of March; but no such permission from the Mayor shall be construed to incur on the part of the City any liability for damages by reason of any accident caused by such firing. [*As amended by Ordinance approved July 3, 1867.*]

SEC. 21. Every building hereafter erected, more than one story in height, shall have a scuttle through the roof, and a convenient stairway leading to the same.

SEC. 22. There shall not be kept in any house, or its appurtenances, within the limits of the City, except in a magazine, to be approved by the Fire Marshal, at any one time, more than twenty-eight pounds of gunpowder, which shall be secured in metal canisters, with metal stoppers or covers; and no one canister shall contain more than seven pounds. Any gunpowder kept contrary to this Section, shall be seized by the Fire Marshal, and on conviction, before the Recorder's Court, of the party so keeping the same, it shall be forfeited to the use and benefit of the City, to be sold under the direction of the Mayor, and the offender shall be punished as hereinafter provided.

SEC. 23. Persons carrying gunpowder through the City, to or from the magazine, shall secure the casks in which the same is contained, by good canvas, tow cloth, or leathern bags.

SEC. 24. The Fire Marshal shall have the right and power, and it is hereby made his duty, at such times as he may deem it necessary, between sunrise and sunset, to enter any and all buildings and enclosures, to discover whether the same are in a dangerous state, and if they are, to cause such to be put in a safe condition; he shall also have the power, and it is hereby made his duty, to see that all chimneys, hearths, fire-places, fire-arches, ovens, stove pipes, boilers, kettles, or any structure or apparatus that may be dangerous in causing or promoting fires, are constructed in such a manner as to secure the greatest protection against fire; he shall also have power, and it is hereby made his duty, to require of the owner or occupant of any blacksmith's shop, furnace, foundry, or other manufactory, to erect, alter, or reconstruct his chimney, so as to prevent sparks from passing into the open air; every person who shall neglect, for forty-eight hours after being notified, in writing, or otherwise, by the Fire Marshal, to comply with the requirements provided herein, shall be punished as hereinafter provided.

SEC. 25. It shall be the duty of the Fire Marshal, and Constables of the City, to make complaint for any violation of the provisions of this Ordinance, and their neglect or refusal to do so, shall be sufficient cause for their removal from office.

SEC. 26. Any violation of, or failure to comply with the provisions or requirements of this Ordinance, shall be punished by a fine not to exceed three hundred dollars, and costs; and in the imposition of any such fine and costs, the Court may make a further sentence, that the offender be imprisoned in the Detroit House of Correction, or the County Jail, until such fine and costs be paid: *Provided, however*, That the term of such imprisonment shall not exceed the period of six months.

CHAPTER 86.

INFLAMMABLE GOODS.

[Ordinance approved April 30, 1866.]

SEC. 1. No person or persons shall keep within the limits of the City of Detroit, petroleum to an amount exceeding two barrels, except as hereinafter provided.

SEC. 2. Warehouses or storehouses for the storage of petroleum, naphtha, benzine, and other like inflammable goods, shall not be erected or used within the City limits, except of such construction and in such localities as may be approved by the Fire Marshal and Committee on Fire Department, and their permission in writing obtained. Such buildings shall not be erected in any locality where the same will endanger the property of the locality.

SEC. 3. No person or persons shall keep within the limits of the City of Detroit, naphtha, benzine, or other like inflammable goods, to an amount exceeding one barrel, except in such place or places as shall be designated by the Fire Marshal and Committee on Fire Limits. They shall also keep said articles in metallic vessels, and in a secure place away from fire or any burning light. [*As amended by Ordinance approved March 7, 1870.*]

SEC. 4. No railroad company shall be allowed to receive in or ship from their regular freight warehouses or depots, any petroleum, naphtha, or benzine, but shall erect a special warehouse or depot for the reception, storage and shipment of the above, at a suitable place on their track, the location to be approved by the Fire Marshal and the Committee on Fire Department.

SEC. 5. The introduction of nitro-glycerine within the City limits is hereby prohibited, and any person or persons having the same in their possession shall be liable to the penalties of this Ordinance.

SEC. 6. Any person or persons violating or refusing to comply with the provisions of this Ordinance upon receiving a notice in writing, or otherwise, from the Fire Marshal or any member of the Metropolitan Police, shall, on conviction thereof in the Recorder's Court, be subject to a fine not exceeding one hundred dollars and costs, or in default of payment, be imprisoned in the Detroit House of Correction for a period not exceeding six months. [*As amended by Ordinance approved March 7, 1870.*]

CHAPTER 87.

HOISTWAYS.

[Chapter Thirty-six of the Revised Ordinances of 1863.]

SECTION 1. The owner or occupant of any building in which there is a hoistway, shall cause the same, in each story, to be enclosed by a good and sufficient railing, except when in actual use, and provide for the closing of such hoistways by a trap door, to be closed at the conclusion of the business of each day.

SEC. 2. It shall be the duty of the Fire Marshal to examine into all violations of the preceding section, and make complaints for the same.

SEC. 3. Any violation of this Ordinance shall be punished by a fine not to exceed fifty dollars; and in the imposition of any such fine, the Court may make a further sentence, that the offender be imprisoned until such fine be paid: *Provided, however,* That the period of such imprisonment shall not exceed six months.

TITLE XI.

RESTRAINING ANIMALS.

CHAPTER 88.

PUBLIC POUNDS.

[Ordinance approved March 24, 1870.]

SECTION 1. There shall be two or more public Pounds in the City of Detroit, to be located in such places as may be designated by the Common Council, and which shall be kept open between the first day of April and the first day of December in each year.

SEC. 2. Pound Masters shall be appointed by the Common Council, and shall hold their offices for the period of eight months, and shall receive for their services the sum of sixty dollars per month.

SEC. 3. No horse, ass, mule, swine, sheep, goat or other cattle, and no geese or domestic fowls, shall run at large within such limits of the City of Detroit as may, from time to time, be designated by the Common Council, by resolution.

SEC. 4. It is hereby made the duty of the Pound Master, policemen and constables, and it shall be lawful for any other person of the age of eighteen years and over, to take up and convey to one of the public Pounds any animal or domestic fowl which may be found running at large within such limits of the City as may be designated by the Council; and for such service the person performing it shall receive from the City treasury the following compensation: For taking to a Pound any horse, ass, mule or swine, one dollar a head; any cattle, fifty cents a head; for any sheep or goat, twenty-five cents; for any goose or other domestic fowl, ten cents: *Provided,* That when such service is performed by policemen, no compensation shall be paid therefor. [*As amended by Ordinance approved May 4, 1870.*]

SEC. 5. The Pound Masters shall receive, keep and feed any animal or fowl which may be brought to the Pound.

SEC. 6. The Pound Masters shall record, in a book to be kept for that purpose, and which shall at all times be open for public inspection, the time when any animal or fowl was received, the names of persons bringing such animals or fowls to the pounds, the date and place where such animals were found, the number of all animals or fowls redeemed or sold by him, and to whom sold, and the amount received for each animal or fowl redeemed. He shall not pay any money to persons bringing animals or fowls to the Pound, but instead thereof shall give a certificate to such persons to the City Controller, containing the name of the finder, the amount due, a description of the animals, and the place where found. The person or persons to whom said certificates are given, shall thereupon make affidavit before the Controller, that the facts set forth in said certificate are true, and thereupon the Controller may approve and allow the same, and report to the Council.

SEC. 7. The Pound Master shall, on Saturday of each week, at the public Pounds, sell at public auction any horse, ass, ox or cow which has been impounded therein for a period of six days, and all other animals and fowls which have been impounded therein for a period of three days, and are unclaimed, or whose owners refuse to pay the fees hereinafter provided. Notice of such sale shall be given at least three days prior thereto, and shall contain a description, as near as may be, of the animal or fowl to be sold, and shall be posted in conspicuous positions in the three following places, to wit: At the City Hall, the County Court House, and the Pound where such sale is to be held.

SEC. 8. The proceeds arising from the sale of any animal or fowl, and all fees received by the Pound Masters, shall, on Monday of each week, be paid into the City Treasury, and a receipt taken for the same. After deducting all lawful fees and costs, the money paid into the Treasury for the sale of any animal or fowl shall be delivered to the former owner of such animal or fowl, on satisfactory proof to the Treasurer that he or she was such owner: *Provided,* That all money deposited as aforesaid, which may remain unclaimed for the period of one year, shall be transferred and credited by the Treasurer to the General Fund.

SEC. 9. He shall also, on Monday of each week, make a report to the City Controller, certified to by the affidavit of said Pound Master, of all animals impounded during the week, by whom they were brought, and where they were found, the number redeemed or sold, the number remaining in the Pound, the amount of money received for each animal redeemed or sold, together with the receipt from the City Treasurer of the amount of money paid into the Treasurer's office by the said Pound Master; and the Controller shall thereupon file and keep the same in his office.

SEC. 10. The Controller shall also furnish the Pound Masters with all necessary books and papers, and shall purchase all necessary supplies for the sustenance of all animals and fowls impounded; and he shall examine the books of the Pound Masters once in each month during the season.

SEC. 11. Pound Masters shall demand and receive the following fees for the benefit of the City of Detroit: For receiving and discharging or selling any horse, ass, mule, swine or ox, two dollars; any calf, cow, sheep or goat, one dollar; for keeping and feeding any horse, ass, mule, swine or ox, one dollar a day; any sheep, goat, cow or calf, twenty-five cents a day; for receiving and discharging any goose or fowl, ten cents, and for keeping any domestic fowl, ten cents a day: *Provided,* When animals or fowls are redeemed within six hours after they are impounded, the Pound Master shall not demand or receive compensation for keeping or feeding.

SEC. 12. In no case shall the Pound Master receive any animals or fowls brought to the Pound that were found outside the limits designated by the Common Council, except in cases where private damages were sustained.

SEC. 13. In no case shall the Pound Master deliver to any person any animal or fowl lawfully impounded before receiving the established fees, except by order of the Common Council.

SEC. 14. Each Pound Master shall place a sign on his office door, with his name, number and street of his residence thereon; and shall, during business hours, be found at his office.

SEC. 15. No person shall hinder, delay or interfere with any one who is driving or carrying any animal or fowl to the public Pound.

SEC. 16. No person shall break, or attempt to break, or assist in breaking into any Pound.

SEC. 17. No person shall take up, drive or carry to the public Pound any animal or fowl not legally liable to be impounded therein.

SEC. 18. All complaints against the Pound Masters shall be in writing, and be investigated by the Committee on Pounds. The complaint and the testimony taken before the Committee, with their opinion thereon, shall be reported to the Common Council, who shall take such action as the facts warrant.

SEC. 19. The Pound Master shall not receive any other compensation than that herein provided. They may be removed at any time by the Common Council.

SEC. 20. If any animal or fowl that may have been lawfully impounded, shall escape, or be rescued, any Pound Master or policeman may, within seven days thereafter, retake such animal or fowl, and the same may be held and sold, as if no escape or rescue had taken place.

SEC. 21. Any violation of the provisions of this Ordinance shall be punished by a fine not to exceed one hundred dollars, and costs; and in the imposition of such fine and costs, the Court may make a further sentence, that the offender be committed to the County Jail or Detroit House of Correction, until the payment thereof, for any period of time not exceeding six months.

CHAPTER 89.

DOGS.

[Chapter Eighty-four of the Revised Ordinances of 1863.]

SECTION 1. Upon each dog in this City a tax of two dollars per annum shall be paid by its owner or possessor, to be levied and collected in the same manner as other City taxes, upon personal property.

SEC. 2. The owner or possessor of any dog, shall put around the neck of the same a collar, upon which shall be engraved, or marked, the name of the owner or possessor.

SEC. 3. Any person who shall suffer to be, or remain in or about the premises occupied by him or her, or to run at large, any dog not having a collar thereon, as required by section two of this Ordinance, may be punished as hereinafter provided.

SEC. 4. It shall be the duty of each member of the Metropolitan Police force, to kill, by shooting or otherwise, any dog, slut or bitch, found or met going at large, unless such dog shall be well and sufficiently muzzled, so as to render it impossible for such dog, slut or bitch to bite or snap at any person ; and further, that any citizen over twenty-one years of age, who shall be thereto authorized, in writing, by the Mayor, may also shoot or otherwise destroy any dog, slut or bitch so found going at large and not so muzzled. [*As amended by Ordinance approved June 19, 1867.*]

SEC. 5. It shall be the duty of the Metropolitan Police, Constables, and such person or persons as may be authorized by the Common Council, and it shall be lawful for any persons, to take up and impound any dog found at large without a collar.

SEC. 6. Any person who shall permit or suffer his or her dog to be at large between the first day of May and the first day of October, without a good and sufficient muzzle, rendering it impossible for such dog to bite or snap, shall be punished as hereinafter provided.

SEC. 7. It shall be the duty of the Metropolitan Police, and such person or persons as may be authorized by the Common Council, and it shall be lawful for any person, to take up and impound any dog found at large between the first day of May and the first day of October, without a good and sufficient muzzle, rendering it impossible for such dog to bite or snap.

SEC. 8. The Common Council shall provide a suitable place to be used as a dog pound, in which all dogs found running at large, contrary to the provisions of this Ordinance, shall be impounded. Such pound shall be provided with a suitable vat or basin, in which all dogs unreclaimed, as provided in the next section, shall be drowned.

SEC. 9. At the setting of the sun, on each day, all dogs which have been twenty-four hours impounded, under the provisions of this Ordinance, and unreclaimed, shall be drowned, and their bodies buried by the City Scavenger, at the expense of the City.

SEC. 10. The Pound Master of the Pound where the dog pound is located, shall have charge and control of the same; and the owner may reclaim any dog impounded, on paying to said Pound Master, for the benefit of the City, the sum of one dollar.

SEC. 11. The Pound Master shall, on Saturday in each week, pay into the City Treasury all moneys by him received under this Ordinance, and shall at the same time report, under oath, to the City Controller, the number of dogs impounded since his last report, the number reclaimed, the number drowned, and the amount of fees received.

SEC. 12. If any owner or possessor of a fierce or vicious dog shall permit the same to go at large, without being provided with a good and sufficient muzzle, rendering it impossible for such dog to bite or snap, he or she shall be punished as hereinafter provided.

SEC. 13. Any owner or possessor of a female dog, who shall allow the same to run at large while in heat, shall be punished as hereinafter provided, and it shall be the duty of the Metropolitan Police to cause any female dog, so running at large, to be slain.

SEC. 14. Any person violating or failing to comply with the

provisions of this Ordinance, shall be punished by a fine not to exceed one hundred dollars, and costs; and in the imposition of any such fine and costs, the Court may make a further sentence, that the offenders be imprisoned in the Detroit House of Correction until the payment thereof, for any term not exceeding six months.

TITLE XII.

HACKS, DRAYS AND PORTERS.

CHAPTER 90.

PUBLIC CARRIAGES.

[Chapter Eighty-five of the Revised Ordinances of 1863.]

SECTION 1. No person shall keep for hire, within the limits of the City of Detroit, any public carriage, cab, hackney coach, omnibus, or other vehicle, without a license therefor from the Mayor.

SEC. 2. The Mayor is hereby authorized to grant licenses, for the purpose aforesaid, to any resident of the City of Detroit, and a citizen of the United States, of the age of twenty-one years or upwards, of good moral character, upon his paying into the City Treasury the sum of five dollars, for each carriage, cab, hackney coach, omnibus, or other vehicle, to be kept, as aforesaid, for a public conveyance, and executing a bond to the City of Detroit, in the penal sum of one hundred dollars, with sureties, conditioned as provided in power sixty-three, of Chapter five, of the City Charter.

SEC. 3. No person shall drive, or be permitted to drive, any public carriage, cab, hackney coach, omnibus, or other public vehicle, without being licensed as a public driver by the Mayor.

SEC. 4. The Mayor is hereby authorized to grant licenses to residents of Detroit, of the age of twenty-one years and upwards, of good moral character, to act as drivers of public carriages, cabs, hackney coaches, omnibuses, or other vehicles, on the person applying for such license paying into the City Treasury the sum of one dollar, and executing a bond to the City of Detroit, in the penal sum of fifty dollars, with sureties, conditioned as prescribed in power sixty-three, of Chapter five, of the City Charter.

SEC. 5. Every conveyance licensed under this Ordinance, when driven or used at night, shall be provided with two lighted lamps, with plain glass fronts and sides, and having the number of the license of each conveyance painted in legible characters thereon, to be placed in conspicuous places on the outside of such conveyance, in such a manner that the same may be distinctly seen and read when the conveyance is standing or in motion.

SEC. 6. Every person licensed under this Ordinance to keep a public conveyance, shall, at all times, keep a good and sufficient carriage and horses.

SEC. 7. No owner or driver of any public conveyance, while waiting for employment, shall refuse or neglect, when applied to, to convey any person or persons to any place or places within the City of Detroit; and on the person or persons being placed in such conveyance, the same shall be driven by the most direct and safe route to the place to which such person or persons wish to go, and not elsewhere; and no driver or owner of any conveyance, except omnibuses, shall, without the consent of the person or persons therein, or of the person who first engaged such conveyance, place therein any other person or persons.

SEC. 8. No owner or driver of any public conveyance shall suffer the same to remain in any street, square, lane or alley, without some proper person to take care of the same. And no owner or driver of any public conveyance, while waiting for employment on any street or dock, shall snap or flourish his whip, or be guilty of any rude or boisterous conduct or language.

SEC. 9. Every driver of any public conveyance, while the same is waiting for employment, shall remain on or near to the same, and shall so keep his carriage and horses that the same shall not obstruct the travel on any street, avenue or cross-walk.

SEC. 10. No person, unless licensed as an owner or driver, as herein provided, shall procure passengers for, or charge or receive any fare for any public conveyance; and not more than one licensed person shall take charge of, or ride on or in any such conveyance.

SEC. 11. The drivers or owners of public conveyances may demand and receive, for conveying passengers, the following rates or prices of fare, and no more, to wit: For carrying a passenger from one place to another, within the limits of said City, fifty cents; children under ten years of age, not exceeding two in number, when accompanied by parents or guardians, shall be carried free of charge; those in excess of that number shall each be charged half fare. For the use of any public conveyance by the hour, for not more than four persons, and with the privilege of going from place to place, and stopping as often as required, one dollar and fifty cents per hour for the first hour, and one dollar for each additional hour, and for fractional hours at the rate of one dollar per hour; and for each additional passenger twenty-five cents per hour; for the use, by the day, of such conveyance, five dollars; for each trunk, fifteen cents; but no charge shall be made for any bag, valise or bundle, weighing less than fifty pounds.

SEC. 12. When a public conveyance is used between the hours of 11 P. M. and 5. A. M., it shall be lawful to demand and receive, for the same services, one-half more than the rates prescribed above. Any disagreement as to time and rates, shall be determined by the Mayor. [*As amended by Ordinance approved June 24, 1864.*]

SEC. 13. This Ordinance shall apply to any carriage which may at any time be placed on a public stand, for public hire, and to all omnibuses or carriages kept by hotel keepers, for the purpose of conveying passengers, for hire, to and from steamboats and railroad depots, or other places, in said City.

SEC. 14. Any violation of, or failure to comply with the provisions of this Ordinance, shall be punished by a fine not to exceed one hundred dollars, and costs; and in the imposition of any such fine and costs, the Court may make a further sentence, that in default of the payment thereof, within a time to be fixed in such sentence, the offender be committed to the County Jail, or Detroit House of Correction, for any period of time not exceeding six months.

CHAPTER 91.

DRAYS.

[Chapter Eighty-six of the Revised Ordinances of 1863.]

SECTION 1. Every cart, truck, wagon, dray, or other vehicle having two or more wheels, and drawn by one or more horses or other animals, which shall be kept, used, driven or employed for the transportation or conveyance of anything whatsoever, from place to place, within the City of Detroit, for hire, shall be deemed a "public dray," within the meaning of this Ordinance; and no person shall hire or keep for hire any such public dray, without a license therefor from the Mayor, as hereinafter provided.

SEC. 2. The Mayor is hereby authorized to grant licenses to any resident of the City of Detroit, and who is a citizen of the United States, to keep a public dray, on his paying into the City Treasury the sum specified in section three of this Ordinance, and his executing a bond to the City of Detroit, in the penal sum of fifty dollars, with one or more sureties, conditioned for a faithful observance of the Charter and Ordinances of the City.

SEC. 3. The person applying for a license for a dray designed to carry twenty-five hundred pounds or over, shall pay the sum of ten dollars; and for all other drays, the sum of one dollar.

SEC. 4. Every person, licensed as herein provided, shall cause the number of his license to be painted and kept conspicuously, in plain, legible figures, at least two inches long, upon each side of his dray.

SEC. 5. The owner or driver of a licensed dray, shall be entitled to demand and receive the following compensation, and no more: For removing or transporting furniture a distance of not exceeding one mile, one dollar per load, and ten cents for each additional mile; for conveying any article a distance not exceeding one mile, fifty cents, and ten cents for each additional mile.

All disputes and disagreements as to distance or rates of compensation, between draymen and persons employing them, shall be determined by the Mayor. [*As amended by Ordinance approved August 5, 1864.*]

SEC. 6. No drayman shall be guilty of any deceit or misrepresentation in the execution of his duties.

SEC. 7. No drayman shall cruelly beat or torture any horse or other animal, whether belonging to himself or another.

SEC. 8. The iron tire around the wheel of a dray designed to carry twenty-five hundred pounds or more, shall not be less than three inches in breadth, and the nails with which the tire is nailed or fastened to the wheel, shall be sunk into the iron or tire, so that the nails shall not project beyond the surface thereof.

SEC. 9. No public drayman shall refuse to be employed, unless otherwise actually engaged ; nor shall any public drayman neglect or refuse to carry such a load as can be safely and conveniently stored on his dray, and drawn by his horse or horses, mule or mules.

SEC. 10. A drayman shall be entitled to receive the compensation provided in this Ordinance, immediately on the transportation of his load, and, unless so paid, he may retain the articles or things so transported until the matter is determined by the Mayor, whose decision shall be binding on both parties.

SEC. 11. No drayman or person having a dray in charge, shall drive or back the same on any sidewalk, or stop the same on any cross-walk, so as to obstruct or hinder travel, or place the same crosswise of any street, except in loading and unloading, and not then for a greater length of time than is necessary for such purpose.

SEC. 12. It shall not be lawful for any drayman or other person having charge of a dray, to be away from such dray, while the same is moving or passing along any street or avenue ; and draymen and persons having charge of drays, shall, while waiting for employment, be on or near their drays ; and they shall not snap or flourish their whips, or use any rude or boisterous talk or conversation, so as to be an annoyance to persons passing the street.

SEC. 13. It shall be the duty of the Metropolitan Police to make complaint for any violation of the provisions of this Ordinance.

SEC. 14. Chapter sixty-three, of the Revised Ordinances of 1859, and all Ordinances and parts of Ordinances amendatory thereof, are hereby repealed.

SEC. 15. Any violation of, or failure to comply with the provisions of this Ordinance, shall be punished by a fine not to exceed one hundred dollars, and costs; and in the imposition of any such fine and costs, the Court may make a further sentence, that the offender be committed to the County Jail or Detroit House of Correction until the payment thereof, for any period of time not exceeding six months.

CHAPTER 92.

STANDS OF PUBLIC CARRIAGES, DRAYS, ETC.

[Ordinance approved September 14, 1870.]

SECTION 1. Hereafter all hackney coaches, carriages, cabs, and other vehicles, used for carrying passengers, plying for hire within the limits of the City, shall, while waiting for employment, occupy the following stands, and no others, that is to say: The center of Jefferson avenue, from a point fifteen feet easterly of the east line of Woodward avenue to a point fifteen feet westerly of the west line of Bates street; the center of Jefferson avenue, from a point fifteen feet westerly of the west line of Woodward avenue, to a point fifteen feet easterly of the east line of Griswold street; the center of Woodward avenue from a point fifteen feet northerly of the north line of Jefferson avenue to a point fifteen feet southerly of the south line of Larned street; the center of Woodward avenue from a point fifteen feet northerly of the north line of Congress street, to a point fifteen feet southerly of the south line of Michigan avenue.

SEC. 2. All drays, carts, express wagons, and other vehicles used for the transportation of baggage, goods, merchandise and other wares, plying for hire within the limits of the City, shall, while waiting for employment, occupy the following stands, that is to say: The center of Jefferson avenue, between Griswold and Wayne streets; the center of Front street, from Buckley's warehouse to Third street; the center of Jefferson avenue, between Bates and Brush streets; the centre of Woodward avenue between Larned and Congress streets; the center of Woodward avenue, from Jefferson avenue to the river; the north side of Monroe avenue, from Woodward avenue to Farmer street; the north side of Atwater street, commencing at a point forty (40) feet west of Brush street, and extending to Randolph street, to be occupied by drays exclusively; the west side of Brush street, commencing at a point fifty (50) feet north of Atwater street, and extending to Woodbridge street, to be occupied exclusively by city express wagons; *Provided*, That all drays or express wagons standing on Brush or Atwater streets, shall stand in a line parallel with the street, and as near as possible to the sidewalk, so as not to incommode the ordinary travel in the street, and subject to the rights of owners or tenants of property adjacent; and also provided, that none of the said vehicles shall stand within ten feet of any cross-street or cross-walk.

SEC. 3. The driver of any carriage, cart or other vehicle mentioned in this Ordinance, shall, while waiting for employment as aforesaid, remain upon his said vehicle.

SEC. 4. The said vehicles, while occupying the stands aforesaid, shall stand in the centre of said streets, and in a line parallel with the course of said streets; *Provided*, That in all streets where railway tracks are laid down, said vehicles shall so stand as not to interfere with said tracks.

SEC. 5. Any person violating any of the provisions of this Ordinance, shall, for each offense, upon conviction before the Recorder's Court, be punished by a fine not to exceed fifty dollars and costs of prosecution; and in the imposition of any such fine and costs, the Court may make a further sentence that the offender be committed to the House of Correction until the payment thereof, for any period of time not exceeding six months.

CHAPTER 93.

PORTERS AND RUNNERS.

[Chapter Eighty-eight of the Revised Ordinances of 1863.]

SECTION 1. The Mayor of the City of Detroit, for the time being, shall have power, from time to time, to issue licenses, under his hand and seal, to so many and to such persons as he shall think proper, to carry on the business of public porters or runners for hotels, and all omnibus agents, omnibus drivers, and drivers of baggage, and all other persons when acting as porters or runners for hotels; and the Mayor or Recorder, or any three Alderman of the City, shall have power to revoke all or any of such licenses.

SEC. 2. All such licenses shall expire on the first day of August next after the date thereof, and may be renewed on application of the holders thereof.

SEC. 3. For every such license shall be paid, by the person applying for the same, the sum of one dollar, and for every renewal, the same sum.

SEC. 4. No person, while acting in the capacity of a public porter or runner for any hotel, or as an omnibus agent, omnibus driver, or driver of a baggage wagon, shall in any manner tease, vex or annoy passengers in soliciting patronage for their respective hotels or conveyances by following after, surrounding, obstructing or in any manner interfering with a quiet and undisturbed egress or departure of any and all passengers from the several railroad depots and depot grounds, or from any wharf of said City upon the arrival of any steamboat therein. [*As amended by Ordinance approved July 5, 1867.*]

SEC. 5. Every public porter or runner, omnibus agent, omnibus driver and baggage driver, and every other person acting as runner for hotels, shall wear a badge on his hat, and in a conspicuous place on his body, on which shall be legibly and plainly engraved or printed, his name and the number of his license, under a penalty not to exceed five dollars, in the discretion of the Court, and the costs of prosecution, for each neglect of the provisions of this section.

SEC. 6. Every public porter or runner, omnibus agent, omnibus driver or baggage driver, and every other person acting as porter or runner for hotels, shall have, on a card or plate, printed or engraved, his name and the number of his license, and also the prices or rates of fare allowed by law for omnibuses, hackney coaches, etc., in legible characters, which shall be nailed on a conspicuous part of his carriage, omnibus, wagon, sleigh, wheelbarrow or hand cart, under a penalty not to exceed five dollars, in the discretion of the Court, and the costs of prosecution, for every violation of the provisions of this section.

SEC. 7. Every person to whom such licenses shall be granted, shall first execute to the City of Detroit, a bond, with one or more sufficient sureties, to be approved by the Mayor, in the penalty of five hundred dollars, conditioned that he will conduct himself in a decent and orderly manner while acting as such porter, runner, omnibus agent, omnibus driver, or driver of baggage, when acting as porter or runner for hotels, and in all respects comply with the provisions of this Ordinance: *Provided, however*, That it shall be lawful for such sureties, or either of them, to vacate such bond by giving ten days' notice, in writing, to the Mayor; and in such case, the said license shall be annulled and made void, unless other sureties are furnished as above provided.

SEC. 8. No porter, runner, hackmen, draymen, City expressmen, omnibus agent, omnibus driver, driver of baggage, or other persons acting as porters or runners for hotels, so licensed as aforesaid, shall, on the arrival of any steamboat or railroad cars in the City of Detroit, for a period of fifteen minutes thereafter, go upon or approach within twenty feet of the wharf or depot where such steamboat or railroad cars have made fast or stopped running, or are about to make fast or stop running, unless such porter, runner, hackmen, draymen, City expressmen, omnibus agent, omnibus driver, or driver of baggage, be requested by a passenger to remove some trunk or other baggage from said wharf or depot, in which case it shall be lawful to go near, in or upon such steamboat or depot for such purpose, under a penalty not to exceed five dollars, in the discretion of the Court, and costs of prosecution, for every such offense.

SEC. 9. No person shall act as porter or runner, or omnibus agent, omnibus driver or baggage driver, when acting as runner or porter for any public house or hotel in the City of Detroit, without being duly licensed, according to the provisions of this Ordinance, under a penalty not to exceed twenty-five dollars, in the discretion of the Court, for every such offense.

SEC. 10. On conviction of any porter, runner, omnibus agent, omnibus driver, or baggage driver, or other person acting as porter or runner for any hotel or public house, licensed as aforesaid, before the Recorder's Court, of any violation of the provisions of this Ordinance, the Mayor or Recorder shall, in his discretion, be authorized, in addition to the fines hereinbefore provided, to vacate and annul any such license that may then be held by any such porter, runner, omnibus agent, omnibus driver or driver of baggage, and to declare the bond of such person forfeited.

SEC. 11. On the forfeiture of the bond of any such porter, runner, omnibus agent, omnibus driver, driver of baggage, or other person, as provided in the preceding section, it shall be the duty of the City Attorney to prosecute the principal and sureties named in such bond, for the benefit of the City.

SEC. 12. Any violation of the provisions of this Ordinance shall be punished by a fine not to exceed one hundred dollars, and the costs of prosecution; and in the imposition of any fine and costs, the Court may make a further sentence, that the offender be imprisoned in the Wayne County Jail or the Detroit House of Correction, until the payment thereof: *Provided, however,* That the period of such imprisonment shall not exceed the term of six months. [*Added by Ordinance approved July 5, 1867.*]

TITLE XIII.

PLACES OF AMUSEMENT AND RECREATION.

CHAPTER 94.

BALL ALLEYS, BILLIARD TABLES, ETC.

[Chapter Eighty-nine of the Revised Ordinances of 1863.]

SECTION 1. No person shall keep a billiard table, nine or ten pin alley, without a license from the Mayor.

SEC. 2. A keeper of a billiard table is one who owns, possesses or keeps a billiard table whereon others are permitted to play, and for which any money or its equivalent, or any check or counter in lieu of money, is paid or received.

SEC. 3. A keeper of a nine or ten pin alley is one who owns, possesses or keeps a ball alley on which persons are permitted to play, and for which money or its equivalent, or any check or counter in lieu of money, is paid or received.

SEC. 4. The Mayor is hereby authorized to grant a license to any person to keep a billiard table, nine or ten pin alley, on the payment of five dollars for each table or alley proposed to be kept by such person, and his executing a bond to the Corporation, in the sum of one hundred dollars with one or more sufficient sureties, conditioned that such person will faithfully observe the Charter and Ordinances of the City.

SEC. 5. Any violation of the provisions of this Ordinance, shall be punished by a fine not to exceed one hundred dollars, and costs; and in the imposition of any such fine and costs, the Court may make a further sentence, that in default of the payment thereof, within a time to be fixed in such sentence, the offender be committed to the County Jail or Detroit House of Correction, for any period of time not exceeding six months.

CHAPTER 95.

SHOWS.

[Chapter Ninty-one of the Revised Ordinances of 1863.]

SECTION 1. No person or persons, company or companies, shall make or exhibit, in said City, any circus, menagerie, play, game, or theatrical exhibition; or give any concert, vocal or instrumental; or exhibit any natural or artificial curiosity; or give any public entertainment or amusement of any kind, for which pay is demanded or received, without a license from the Mayor.

SEC. 2. The Mayor is hereby authorized to grant licenses for the purposes aforesaid, on the payment of such sum of money as may be previously determined upon by himself and the Committee on Licenses.

SEC. 3. This Ordinance shall not extend to any exhibition by the pupils of any private or public School, or to any exhibition of painting, engraving, sculpture or fine art, executed by a citizen of Detroit, or to any concert or musical entertainment for the benefit of any Church or benovelent object.

SEC. 4. It shall be the duty of any person or company receiving a license, to keep good order in and about his or their place of amusement or exhibition; and for that purpose, to keep at his or their expense a sufficient police force thereat.

SEC. 5. Any violation of this Ordinance, shall be punished by a fine not to exceed the sum of two hundred dollars, and by imprisonment in the County Jail or Detroit House of Correction, for a period not exceeding six months, or either, in the discretion of the Court; and in the imposition of a fine only, the Court may make a further sentence, that the offender be imprisoned until such fine be paid; but for a time not exceeding that provided herein.

TITLE XIV.

LICENSES.

CHAPTER 96.

LICENSES.

[Chapter Ninety-seven of the Revised Ordinances of 1863.]

SECTION 1. In all cases, unless otherwise provided, where, by Ordinance or Resolution of the Common Council, a sum of money is fixed for the payment of a license, it shall be understood to be for the period of one year, and, except as provided in the next section, all licenses shall expire on the first day of August next after the date thereof.

SEC. 2. For good cause shown, the Mayor is hereby authorized to grant licenses, in all cases where the price of the licenses amounts to five dollars or more, for any period not less than three months, on the payment of a sum proportioned to the time for which any such license is granted. The amount required to be paid for any license so issued, shall be paid to and collected by the Collector, and the receipt of such Collector shall be taken and received by the Mayor as evidence of the payment of the same. [*As amended by Ordinance approved October 10, 1863.*]

SEC. 3. All licenses shall be revocable at the pleasure of the Mayor or Common Council, but no license granted under any Ordinance or Resolution of the Common Council, shall be assignable; but for the promotion of the ends of justice, the Mayor is hereby authorized, with the consent of the parties, to transfer a license from one person to another, on the transferee executing a bond to the Corporation, as provided in the Charter and Ordinances of the City for persons receiving licenses.

SEC. 4. All licenses granted under any Resolution or Ordinance of the Common Council, shall be signed by the Mayor and countersigned by the Clerk of the City, who shall keep, in books to be provided therefor, full minutes of the same, and of all transfers thereof, and, as near as may be, shall be in the following form:

"CITY OF DETROIT:—I, ——, Mayor of the City of Detroit.
To all who shall see these presents—Greeting:

"Know ye, that —— has paid into the Treasury of the City the sum of —— dollars, and otherwise complied with the provisions of the Charter and Ordinances of the City in this behalf; therefore, the said —— is hereby authorized and empowered to —— for the period of —— months from the date hereof.

[L. S.] "In witness whereof, I have hereunto set my hand, and caused the seal of the City to be affixed, at the City Hall in said City, this —— day of ——, A. D. 18—.

——, *Mayor.*

"Countersigned, ——, *City Clerk.*"

TITLE XV.

MISCELLANEOUS.

CHAPTER 97.

EXTENDING LIMITS OF THE THIRD WARD.

[Chapter Ninety-six of the Revised Ordinances of 1863.]

SECTION. 1. The limits of the Third Ward of said City shall be, and hereby are extended to Gratiot street, by adding to said Third Ward, and incorporating as part of the same, all that portion of the Sixth Ward in said City bounded as follows, to wit: On the south by Croghan street, on the west by Randolph street, on the north by Gratiot street, and on the east by St. Antoine street, and by a line on the course of St. Antoine street, if extended from Clinton street to Gratiot street.

SEC. 2. Nothing in this Ordinance contained shall be construed to affect the basis of taxation in the Sixth or in the Third Ward, aforesaid, during the present year, or to affect or remove from office any officer continued in office by the Revised Charter of the present year, during the time for which said person is so continued in office.

CHAPTER 98.

ELECTION DISTRICTS—FIFTH AND SIXTH WARDS.

[Ordinance approved August 8, 1868.]

SECTION 1. That hereafter each of the following wards, to wit: The Fifth and Sixth Wards in the City of Detroit, be and the same is hereby divided into two election districts.

SEC. 2. The First Election District of said Fifth Ward shall comprise all that portion of said Ward bounded as follows, to wit: Commencing at the intersection of Woodward and Michigan avenues, and running thence west to the east line of the Forsyth farm; thence north 22° 47′ west to the center of Orchard street; thence north 67° 13′ east to Grand River street; thence north 60° east along the center of Elizabeth street, to the center of Woodward avenue; thence south 30° east along the center of Woodward avenue, to the place of beginning.

And the Second Election District shall comprise all that portion of said Ward bounded as follows, to wit: Commencing at the intersection of the center of Woodward avenue and Elizabeth street, running thence north 26° 19′ east along the center of Woodward avenue, to the northerly line of the City; thence south 60° west to the easterly line of the Forsyth farm; thence south 22° 47′ east to the center of Orchard street; thence north 67° 13′ east along the center of Orchard street to Grand River; thence north 60° east along the center of Elizabeth street, to the place of beginning. [*As amended by Ordinance approved August 13, 1868.*]

SEC. 3. The First Election District of said Sixth Ward shall comprise all that portion of said Ward bounded as follows, to wit: Commencing at the intersection of the corner of St. Antoine and Gratiot streets, thence north 26° west to the northerly line of the City; thence south 60° west to the center of Woodward avenue; thence south 26° and 19′ east to the northerly line of Adams avenue; thence south 30° east to the centers of Woodward and Monroe avenues; thence north 30° east along the center of Monroe avenue to the center of Randolph street; thence north 26° west to the center of Gratiot street; thence north 29° 47′ east to the place of beginning.

And the Second Election District shall comprise all that portion of said Ward bounded as follows, to wit: Commencing at the intersection of the centers of Gratiot and St. Antoine streets, thence north 26° west to the northerly line of the City; thence north 60° east to the Detroit and Milwaukee Railroad track; thence south 26° east along the line of the Dequindre and

Witherell farms to the center of Gratiot street; thence south 29° and 46′ west to the place of beginning.

SEC. 4. Polling places shall be established by resolution of the Common Council in each of the Election Districts as above divided for the purposes of holding general and special elections; and it shall not be competent for any elector resident in such district to vote at any place other than that so designated or prescribed.

NINTH WARD.

[Ordinance approved August 29, 1870.]

SEC. 5. The First Election District shall comprise all that part of the Ninth Ward west of the east line of the Woodbridge farm, east of the west line of the Godfrey farm, and south of the Detroit & Toledo Railroad track, and north of the Detroit River.

SEC. 6. The Second Election District shall comprise all that part of the Ninth Ward west of the west line of the Godfrey farm, east of the west line of the Porter farm, and south of the Detroit & Toledo Railroad track, and north of the Detroit River.

CHAPTER 99.

EXECUTION OF DEEDS, ETC.

[Ordinance approved May 12, 1865.]

SECTION 1. Whenever the Common Council shall direct that any deed, conveyance or other instrument under seal shall be executed by or on behalf of the City of Detroit, the same shall be executed by the Mayor and Controller signing the same, and by affixing thereto the seal of said City of Detroit, attested by the City Clerk. It shall be the duty of said Mayor, Controller and Clerk to, in all cases, comply with the intent of this section.

CHAPTER 100.

THE PAYMENT OF CLAIMS AND DEMANDS AGAINST THE CITY OF DETROIT.

[Chapter Ninety-eight of the Revised Ordinances of 1863.]

SECTION. 1. All claims and demands, of every name and nature whatsoever, against the City of Detroit, shall, in the first instance, be presented and filed with the City Controller, who shall present the same to the Common Council, at its next session, or as soon thereafter as practicable, with a communication, in writing, setting forth the facts in relation to such claims and demands, and his opinion in relation to the payment thereof.

SEC. 2. Any unliquidated claim or demand against the City, when presented to the Controller, shall be accompanied with an affidavit of the person rendering it, as provided in section twenty-five, of chapter four, of the Charter of the City of Detroit.

SEC. 3. Any person presenting a claim or demand against the City, for supplies furnished for the use of the Corporation, or any Board thereof, shall accompany the same with a bill of the items thereof, with the name or names of the person or persons upon whose order the same were furnished.

SEC. 4. All claims and demands against the City, for work or labor performed for the Corporation, under any contract for paving any street, lane or alley, or for the construction or repair of any sewer, drain, side or cross-walk, bridge or culvert, shall be accompanied with a written statement, under oath, of the amount of work or labor performed, and the precise locality where such work was performed, and the extent of the same. And before any such claim or demand is presented for allowance to the Common Council, it shall be the duty of the Controller to refer the same to the City Surveyor to ascertain whether such work has been performed agreeably to contract, and in the manner and to the extent set forth in the statement accompanying such claim or demand, and has been performed in other respects in a good, substantial, and workmanlike manner.

SEC. 5. In the allowance of any claim or demand for the payment of which a special assessment has been levied, the Common Council shall not appropriate any money for the payment thereof, except such as shall have been paid into the City Treasury in payment of the assessment levied upon the lot or lots in front of or adjacent to which such work has been performed.

SEC. 6. The Common Council shall not order any warrant to be drawn on the City Treasurer, when the fund out of which such warrant is to be paid has been exhausted.

SEC. 7. It shall be the duty of the Controller, when any claim or demand against the City has been paid, to take a receipt therefor and file the same in his office.

SEC. 8. No claim or demand against the City of Detroit shall be paid until the same has been audited and allowed by the Common Council.

CHAPTER 101.

CANCELING THE ORDERS, WARRANTS AND DUE-BILLS OF THE CITY OF DETROIT.

[Chapter Ninety-nine of the Revised Ordinances of 1863.]

SECTION 1. The City Treasurer, shall, without delay, procure a proper canceling hammer, such as is ordinarily used by banking institutions, with which he shall immediately cut, mark and cancel every order, due-bill, warrant or other evidence of debt issued by the City of Detroit, or by the Common Council of said City, or under their direction, which now are in the City Treasury; and hereafter the said Treasurer shall, as soon as any order, due-bill, or warrant, or other evidence of debt heretofore issued, or which hereafter shall or may at any time or times be issued by said City of Detroit, or by said Common Council, or by or under their direction or authority, shall come or be paid into the Treasury of said City, cut, mark and cancel the same with said canceling hammer.

SEC. 2. After the City Treasurer shall have so cut, marked and canceled said orders, warrants, due-bills, or other evidence of debt, as aforesaid, he shall carefully and safely file and keep the same until the further order or action of said Common Council.

SEC. 3. It shall be the duty of the City Treasurer, from and after the passage of this Chapter, to keep a book or record, in which he shall enter, as soon as he receives the same, the number, date and amount of each and every warrant, order, due-bill and evidence of debt, as aforesaid, received into the City Treasury; and whenever the City Treasurer shall report to said Common Council any amount of warrants, orders, due-bills, or other evidences of debt, as hereinafter provided for, he shall accompany his report with a schedule or list of said warrants, orders, due-bills, or other evidence of debt so reported, with the number, date and amount of each.

SEC. 4. Whenever the City Treasurer shall have in his possession one thousand dollars of cut, marked, and canceled warrants, orders, due-bills, or other evidences of debt, issued, or hereafter to be issued, as aforesaid, he shall report the fact to the said Common Council, whilst in session, and thereupon, at the same session of said Council, or at the next regular meeting, said Council shall cause said orders, due-bills, warrants or other evidences of debt aforesaid, to be carefully examined and checked on the warrant book, in presence of the Council, by a committee of three, to be appointed from time to time, by the Mayor, of whom the Clerk shall be one; and the same having been so counted, examined and checked, shall be forthwith burned, or otherwise destroyed, in the presence of the Council, and the amount so destroyed, with the number or other suitable designation of each, shall be entered on the Journal of the Council.

CHAPTER 102.

PARTITION FENCES.

[Ordinance approved February 8, 1868.]

SECTION 1. The respective owners of all lots in the City of Detroit shall construct and maintain partition fences between their own and the next adjoining lots, at an equal expense to each owner; such partition fence shall be constructed of posts sunk in the soil at least three feet, and of a height above the surface of at least five feet, with rough boards; in all cases when the houses in streets on which lots front run by numbers from east to west, the posts shall be placed contiguous to and on the westerly side of the dividing line, and the boards shall be nailed or fastened to the easterly side of the post; and when the houses on such streets number from west to east, the posts shall be placed on the easterly side of the dividing line, and the boards on the westerly side of the posts; on lots fronting on streets, the numbers of the houses whereon run from north to south, the fence posts shall be placed contiguous to and on the north side of the dividing line, and the boards on the south side of the posts; and when such numbers run from south to north, such posts shall be placed contiguous to and on the south side of the dividing line, and the boards on the north side of the posts.

SEC. 2. Whenever any party shall neglect to build, repair or rebuild any partition fence which of right he ought to build, repair or rebuild, the aggrieved party may complain to the Street Commissioner of the district in which the premises are situated, who shall give notice in writing to the parties of the time and place, when he shall examine into the same; upon such examination, said Commissioner shall determine in writing if such is required to be built, repaired or rebuilt, and in such case the proportion shall be paid by each of the owners; a copy of which shall be served on each party in interest; if any party shall neglect for the space of twenty days, after service of such finding, to comply with the requirements thereof, the other party may proceed to build, repair or rebuild such fence, and the party neglecting to comply with the requirements of such finding, shall be liable to the party doing the work for the entire expense thereof, and also for the expenses of the Commissioner, as hereinafter provided for.

SEC. 3. The party applying to the Commissioner shall pay him for his services the sum of three dollars for each day that he is engaged in the premises; if the parties comply with the finding of the Commissioner, as provided in section two, one-half his fees shall be refunded to the complainant by the other party; but if either shall fail to so comply with the finding, such party shall be liable for all such fees.

SEC. 4. Notwithstanding anything in this Ordinance contained, the owners of adjacent lots may amicably agree upon the size, character and height of their partition fences, and the proportion in which they shall bear the expense thereof.

CHAPTER 103.

INDEXING COUNCIL PROCEEDINGS.

[Ordinance approved October 20, 1870.]

SECTION 1. It shall be the duty of the City Clerk to prepare an index to the printed volume of proceedings of the Common Council of each year, and he shall receive therefor, in addition to his salary, such compensation as shall be fixed by the Common Council.

CHAPTER 104.

UNIFORMITY IN THE NAMES OF STREETS.

[Ordinance approved October 1, 1866.]

SECTION. 1. The street in the Sixth Ward of the City of Detroit, heretofore named and called Earl street, shall be hereafter named and called High treet.

SEC. 2. The street in the Sixth Ward of the City of Detroit, heretofore named and called Warren street, shall be hereafter named and called Napoleon street.

[Ordinance approved July 9, 1867.]

SEC. 3. That Witherell street, from Adams avenue to City limits, be and the same is hereby changed to Woodward avenue.

That Chicago road, from Eighth street to City limits, be and the same is hereby changed to Michigan avenue.

That Cemetery street, in the Sixth Ward, be and the same is hereby changed to High street.

That High street, from Hasting street to McDougall street, be and the same is hereby changed to Sherman street.

That Canfield street, extension of Bagg street, across Cass farm, be and the same is hereby changed to Bagg street.

That Chestnut street, from Forsyth farm west to City limits, be and the same is hereby changed to Canfield street.

That Frasier street, extension of Chestnut street west, across the Guoin farm, be and the same is hereby changed to Chestnut street.

That Waterloo street and the Davidson street extension of Waterloo street, be and the same are hereby changed to Antietam street.

That Elm street, from Riopelle street to Orleans street, be and the same is hereby changed to Marion street.

That Cherry street, from Russell street east to Gratiot street, be and the same is hereby changed to Bronson street.

That Park street, from Lasalle avenue west to Loranger farm, be and the same is hereby changed to Rose street.

That Park street, from Michigan avenue north to Grand River street, be and the same is hereby changed to Park place.

That Pine street, from Hasting street east to Rivard street, be and the same is hereby changed to Guoin street.

That Henry street, from continuation of Howard street west, be and the same is hereby changed to Howard street.

That Stephen street, from continuation of Baker street west, be and the same is hereby changed to Baker street.

That Circus street, from continuation of William street, from Woodward to Adams avenue, be and the same is hereby changed to William street.

That Circus street, from continuation of Park street, from Adams avenue to Woodward avenue, be and the same is hereby changed to Park street.

That State street, from continuation of Gratiot street, from Randolph street to Woodward avenue, be and the same is hereby changed to Gratiot street.

That Chene and Jupiter streets, from east and west half of same street, be and the same are changed to Chene street.

That Mount Elliott and Montgomery avenues be and the same are hereby changed to Mount Elliott avenue.

That Alexander street, across Chene farm, be and the same is hereby changed to Wight street.

That Poplar street, across the west half of Thompson farm, south of Grand River street, be and the same is hereby changed to Grant street.

That Charlotte street, across the Witherell farm, Tenth Ward, be and the same is hereby changed to Witherell street.

That Francis street, across the Witherell farm, Tenth Ward, is hereby changed to Federal street.

That St. Lawrence street, extension of Montcalm street, be and the same is hereby changed to Montcalm street.

That Trumbull avenue, be and the same is hereby changed to Ninth avenue.

That Dudley street be and the same is hereby changed to Tenth street.

That the street running from Fort street to Woodbridge street, parallel with, and on the west line of Woodbridge farm, be and is hereby named Eleventh street.

That Thompson street be and the same is hereby changed to Twelfth street.

That Lafferty street be and the same is hereby changed to Thirteenth street.

That the street known as Peter street, be and the same is hereby changed to Thirteenth-and-one-half street.

That Godfroy avenue be and the same is hereby changed to Fourteenth street.

That Lafontaine avenue be and the same is hereby changed to Fifteenth street.

That the street running from Fort to Woodbridge street, through the center of Lafontaine farm, be and the same is hereby changed to Fifteenth-and-a-half street.

That Lasalle avenue be and the same is hereby changed to Sixteenth street.

That Trowbridge street be and the same is hereby changed to Seventeenth street.

That Stanton street be and the same is hereby changed to Seventeenth-and-a-half street.

That Whiting street be and the same is hereby changed to Eighteenth street.

That Wine street be and the same is hereby changed to Eighteenth-and-a-half street.

That Wing street be and the same is hereby changed to Nineteenth street.

That St. Clair street be and the same is hereby changed to Twentieth street.

That Holbrook street be and the same is hereby changed to Twenty-first street.

That Brevoort street be and the same is hereby changed to Twenty-second street.

That Lyell avenue be and the same is hereby changed to Twenty-fourth street.

That the street known as Porter Road or West avenue, be and

the same is hereby changed to Twenty-fourth street. [*As amended by Ordinance approved April 25, 1868.*]

[Ordinance approved August 25, 1868.]

SEC. 4. That Lafayette street, west, be and the same is hereby changed to Lafayette avenue, and Fourteenth street to Fourteenth avenue.

[Ordinance approved June 14, 1869.]

SEC. 5. That the name of Osceola street be and is hereby changed to Brigham street; that the name of Grand street be and is hereby changed to Alexandrine avenue; that the names of Liberty and Laurel be and are hereby changed to Fulton street; and that the name of Railroad street is hereby changed to Watson street.

[Ordinance approved September 27, 1869.]

SEC. 6. That Limburg street be and is hereby changed to Charlotte avenue, and Trombley street to Harriet street.

[Ordinance approved January 8, 1870.]

SEC. 7. That the name of Private street be and the same is hereby changed to Chase street.

[Ordinance approved February 14, 1870.]

SEC. 8. That the name of Whitney street, in the Sixth Ward of said City, be and the same is hereby changed to Alfred street.

[Ordinance approved March 21, 1870.]

SEC. 9. That the name of Seward street be and the same is hereby changed to Leland street; that the name of Railroad street be and the same is hereby changed to Watson street; that the name of Juliette street be and the same is hereby changed to Wilkins street; that the name of James street be and the same is hereby changed to Alfred street; that the name of North street be and the same is hereby changed to Division street; that the name of Trombley street be and the same is hereby changed to Harriet street; and that the name of Palmer street be and the same is hereby changed to West Park place.

[Ordinance approved June 16, 1870.]

SEC. 10. That the name of Paton alley be and the same is hereby changed to Paton street.

[Ordinance approved June 18, 1870.]

SEC. 11. That the name of Campau street be and the same is hereby changed to McDougall avenue.

CHAPTER 105.

DIRT IN STREETS. *

[Ordinance approved January 28, 1871.]

SECTION 1. No person shall scatter, leave or distribute in any street, lane or alley, or public space within the limits of the City, dirt of any description, carted or hauled about in wagons, and any person using wagons, carts or other vehicles, to haul dirt, shall not load the same above the top of the side or end boards of the same, and any such wagon, cart or vehicle used for the purposes aforesaid, shall be constructed with tight board boxes in such manner as to prevent the distribution or scattering of dirt on the streets.

SEC. 2. Any violation of the provisions of this Ordinance shall be punished by a fine not to exceed one hundred dollars and costs of prosecution; and the offender may be imprisoned in the Detroit House of Correction until the payment thereof: *Provided, however,* That the time of such imprisonment shall not exceed six months.

* This Chapter was enacted after the printing of Title 3.

AN ORDINANCE

TO GIVE EFFECT TO THE REVISED ORDINANCES OF EIGHTEEN HUNDRED AND SEVENTY-ONE.

It is hereby ordained by the Common Council of the City of Detroit:

SECTION 1. That the edition of the Ordinances of the City of Detroit, compiled and published in accordance with the resolution of the Common Council, adopted December 16th, 1870, shall be called "The Revised Ordinances of the City of Detroit for the year 1871," and this Ordinance shall take effect and go into operation from and after the first day of February, 1871.

Approved January 28, 1871.

WILLIAM W. WHEATON,
Mayor.

Attest, HENRY STARKEY,
City Clerk.

INDEX.

www.ingramcontent.com/pod-product-compliance
Lightning Source LLC
LaVergne TN
LVHW010255110826
845151LV00004B/1482

* 9 7 8 1 4 2 5 5 2 2 2 5 4 *